Prepare for Grade 3

Second Edition

Summertime Learning

Prepare Your Child for Third Grade

Directions in Spanish and English

Editorial Project Manager
Eric Migliaccio

Editor in Chief
Brent L. Fox, M. Ed.

Creative Director
Sarah M. Fournier

Cover Artist
Diem Pascarella

Illustrators
Mark Mason
Renée Mc Elwee

Art Coordinator
Renée Mc Elwee

Imaging
Amanda R. Harter

Publisher
Mary D. Smith, M.S. Ed.

Teacher Created Resources
12621 Western Avenue
Garden Grove, CA 92841
www.teachercreated.com

ISBN: 978-1-4206-8087-4

Reprinted, 2023 (PO604798)

Made in U.S.A.

Teacher Created Resources

Table of Contents

Table of Contents *(cont.)*

An Important Message

El siguiente es un mensaje importante de la Asociación Nacional de Aprendizaje de Verano.

Estimados padres,

¿Sabían que todos los jóvenes experimentan una pérdida de aprendizaje cuando no participan en actividades educativas durante el verano? Esto significa que parte de lo aprendido durante el año escolar suele evaporarse durante los meses de verano. Sin embargo, la pérdida de aprendizaje se puede prevenir con la ayuda de los padres. El verano es la época ideal para participar en actividades interesantes y divertidas que ayuden a los niños a conservar y desarrollar sus habilidades académicas. Algunas ideas:

- Lean con sus hijos a diario. Visiten juntos la biblioteca local y escojan libros que aborden temas de su interés.
- Pidan a los docentes recomendaciones para la lectura de verano. The Summer Reading List (páginas 92–93 de esta guía) constituye un buen punto de partida.
- Exploren parques, reservas naturales, museos y centros culturales.
- Consideren cada día como un sinfín de posibilidades de aprendizaje. Medir las cantidades en una receta o estudiar un mapa antes de un viaje en auto constituyen algunos modos de adquirir o reforzar una habilidad. Utilicen las Learning Experiences que se encuentran al final de este libro para obtener más ideas.
- Establezcan metas a alcanzar de forma diaria. Por ejemplo, realizar cinco problemas de Matemáticas o leer un capítulo de un libro.
- Alienten a su hijo a completar las actividades de los libros tales como *Summertime Learning*, con el fin de reducir la brecha de aprendizaje que suele producirse en el verano.

Nuestra visión es que cada niño se sienta seguro, saludable y comprometido con el aprendizaje durante el verano. Para obtener más información, diríjanse a *www.summerlearning.org*.

¡Que pasen un verano *memorable*!

Matthew Boulay
NSLA Founder

Using This Book

Como padre, posiblemente sepas que el verano es una época para divertirse. Pero también puede ser un tiempo para aprender y prepararse para el próximo año escolar. Al combinar la diversión con el aprendizaje, los libros incluidos en la serie *Summertime Learning* pueden ayudar a tu hijo a mantenerse en el camino educativo y, a su vez, disfrutar del descanso físico y mental que tanto necesita. Con el fin de ayudarte a ayudarlo, hemos desarrollado un recurso organizado, flexible, práctico y gratificante.

Organizado

Summertime Learning: Prepare Your Child for Third Grade se encuentra organizado en torno a un período vacacional de ocho semanas. Incluye dos actividades para cada día de la semana. De lunes a jueves, dichas actividades consisten en una lección de Matemáticas y una lección de lectura o escritura. Los viernes ofrecen un divertido cambio de ritmo e incluyen actividades que se centran en habilidades tales como la creatividad, el pensamiento crítico, la capacidad de seguir instrucciones y la resolución de problemas.

Flexible

Hay muchos modos de utilizar este libro de forma efectiva:

- **Día a día**—Tu hijo puede realizar las actividades en orden, comenzando el primer lunes de las vacaciones. Para cada día de la semana, realizará las dos actividades designadas. (Consulta el calendario de la página 7).
- **A elección**—Si no quieres que tu hijo realice las actividades estrictamente en el orden en que están presentadas en el libro, puedes elegir una combinación de páginas acorde con sus necesidades e intereses.
- **De todo tipo**—Si sientes que tu hijo necesita más apoyo en un área que en otra, puedes optar por centrarte en las actividades de Matemáticas o Artes del Lenguaje.

Además, las páginas de este libro se encuentran perforadas, lo que permite arrancarlas en caso de ser necesario. Si se escoge este método, se puede decorar una carpeta y designarla especialmente para almacenar las páginas sueltas.

Extra Extra

- Para acceder a un práctico calendario que ayude a establecer expectativas y mantenerse al día, consulta la página 7 de este libro.

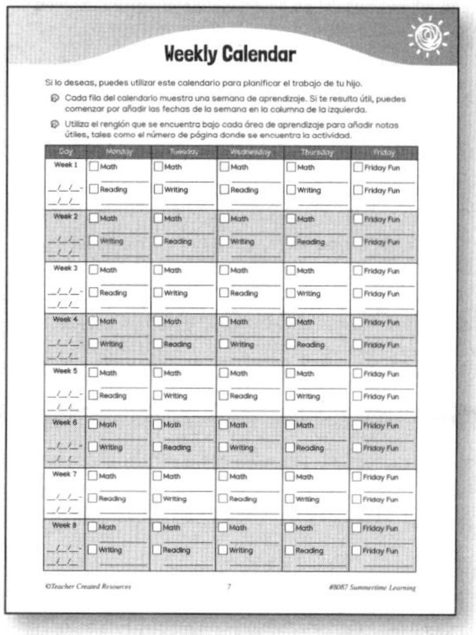

- Para incluir más escritura en el programa semanal, consulta los "Journal Topics" en la página 8.
- Para conocer distintos modos de incrementar la lectura de verano y las experiencias de aprendizaje, consulta las páginas 92–97.
- Para acceder a páginas de referencia útiles en el área de la escritura en cursiva, multiplicación, registro y lectura del tiempo, y más, consulta las páginas 98–104.

Using This Book *(cont.)*

Práctico

Los padres desean páginas de actividades que no generen dudas sobre cómo utilizarlas, qué se espera que su hijo haga, y cuáles son las respuestas correctas. Las páginas de *Summertime Learning: Prepare Your Child for Third Grade* tienen como objetivo responder a esta necesidad.

En la parte superior de cada página de actividades se ofrecen distintos datos de forma directa y de fácil lectura.

1. En un costado de la página de actividades, se encuentran el día de la semana y el área de aprendizaje. Esto permite a los padres verificar rápidamente en qué se encuentra trabajando su hijo y mantenerse organizados a lo largo del verano.
2. En el costado opuesto de la página figura un ícono de un sol. Constituye el sitio ideal para colocar una calcomanía y, de esta forma, hacer un seguimiento del progreso de tu hijo y recompensarlo cuando completa las actividades incluidas en el libro. Esta función también ayudará a orientarlo hacia las actividades del día siguiente: pueden simplemente localizar la última calcomanía colocada y trabajar en las dos páginas consecutivas. Al final del libro, encontrarán más de 300 calcomanías coloridas que podrán ser utilizadas para este fin.
3. Las instrucciones para cada una de las actividades se encuentran escritas de forma clara y de un modo que permita comprenderlas fácilmente. Muchas veces sucede que los niños poseen la capacidad de desempeñar una habilidad educativa, pero responden de modo incorrecto porque las instrucciones no son lo suficientemente claras o no han sido leídas en su totalidad. Puedes alentar a tu hijo a escribir un número sobre cada una de las instrucciones que indiquen una nueva tarea.
4. Algunas páginas incluyen un casillero llamado "What to Know" que ofrece un recordatorio de la regla gramatical u ortográfica que tu hijo deberá saber para poder completar la página.

Además, al final del libro se incluye una guía completa de respuestas (páginas 105–111) que puede ser consultada cada vez que se tengan dudas sobre alguna respuesta.

Recompensas

Puedes utilizar el Reward Chart que se encuentra en la página 112 de este libro para realizar un seguimiento de aquellas actividades que ya han sido completadas. Esta página está diseñada para ser utilizada con las calcomanías proporcionadas al final de este libro. Cada vez que tu hijo finalice una página, puede escoger una calcomanía y utilizarla para rellenar uno de los círculos del gráfico.

Las calcomanías también pueden ser utilizadas en las páginas individuales. El sol que se encuentra en la parte superior de la página constituye el sitio ideal para colocar la calcomanía escogida. De este modo, será más fácil orientarlo hacia las actividades del día siguiente: pueden simplemente localizar la última calcomanía colocada y trabajar en las dos páginas consecutivas.

Weekly Calendar

Si lo deseas, puedes utilizar este calendario para planificar el trabajo de tu hijo.

- Cada fila del calendario muestra una semana de aprendizaje. Si te resulta útil, puedes comenzar por añadir las fechas de la semana en la columna de la izquierda.
- Utiliza el renglón que se encuentra bajo cada área de aprendizaje para añadir notas útiles, tales como el número de página donde se encuentra la actividad.

Day	Monday	Tuesday	Wednesday	Thursday	Friday
Week 1 __/__/__- __/__/__	☐ Math ________ ☐ Reading ________	☐ Math ________ ☐ Writing ________	☐ Math ________ ☐ Reading ________	☐ Math ________ ☐ Writing ________	☐ Friday Fun ________ ☐ Friday Fun ________
Week 2 __/__/__- __/__/__	☐ Math ________ ☐ Writing ________	☐ Math ________ ☐ Reading ________	☐ Math ________ ☐ Writing ________	☐ Math ________ ☐ Reading ________	☐ Friday Fun ________ ☐ Friday Fun ________
Week 3 __/__/__- __/__/__	☐ Math ________ ☐ Reading ________	☐ Math ________ ☐ Writing ________	☐ Math ________ ☐ Reading ________	☐ Math ________ ☐ Writing ________	☐ Friday Fun ________ ☐ Friday Fun ________
Week 4 __/__/__- __/__/__	☐ Math ________ ☐ Writing ________	☐ Math ________ ☐ Reading ________	☐ Math ________ ☐ Writing ________	☐ Math ________ ☐ Reading ________	☐ Friday Fun ________ ☐ Friday Fun ________
Week 5 __/__/__- __/__/__	☐ Math ________ ☐ Reading ________	☐ Math ________ ☐ Writing ________	☐ Math ________ ☐ Reading ________	☐ Math ________ ☐ Writing ________	☐ Friday Fun ________ ☐ Friday Fun ________
Week 6 __/__/__- __/__/__	☐ Math ________ ☐ Writing ________	☐ Math ________ ☐ Reading ________	☐ Math ________ ☐ Writing ________	☐ Math ________ ☐ Reading ________	☐ Friday Fun ________ ☐ Friday Fun ________
Week 7 __/__/__- __/__/__	☐ Math ________ ☐ Reading ________	☐ Math ________ ☐ Writing ________	☐ Math ________ ☐ Reading ________	☐ Math ________ ☐ Writing ________	☐ Friday Fun ________ ☐ Friday Fun ________
Week 8 __/__/__- __/__/__	☐ Math ________ ☐ Writing ________	☐ Math ________ ☐ Reading ________	☐ Math ________ ☐ Writing ________	☐ Math ________ ☐ Reading ________	☐ Friday Fun ________ ☐ Friday Fun ________

Journal Topics

Haga que su hijo elija uno de estos temas del diario dos veces por semana. En un diario o cuaderno, pídales que escriban algunas oraciones en respuesta al tema elegido. Recuérdeles que agreguen suficientes detalles para que otra persona que lea sus respuestas sepa lo siguiente sobre su tema:

Quién · Qué · Cuando · Dónde · Por qué · Cómo

Si lo deseas, puedes utilizar lo siguiente como herramienta de organización. Marca la fecha en que tu hijo completó cada consigna.

#1 the perfect activity to do in the summer Completed: ______________	#2 something amazing that I have seen Completed: ______________	#3 an animal that I would like to have as a pet Completed: ______________
#4 the last time I laughed really hard Completed: ______________	#5 a fictional character I really like Completed: ______________	#6 the best place to go on vacation Completed: ______________
#7 my room Completed: ______________	#8 what makes someone a good friend Completed: ______________	#9 the best things about technology Completed: ______________
#10 what I like to do during the weekend Completed: ______________	#11 my family Completed: ______________	#12 a book I enjoyed reading Completed: ______________
#13 when I am sad Completed: ______________	#14 what I could win an award for Completed: ______________	#15 if I could create another holiday Completed: ______________
#16 one habit I would really like to break Completed: ______________	#17 a food I like to eat Completed: ______________	#18 my favorite person to talk to Completed: ______________

Standards and Skills

Estándares Educativos

Cada una de las actividades incluidas en *Summertime Learning: Prepare Your Child for Third Grade* cumple con uno o más de los estándares educativos nacionales. Para conocer cómo se relacionan específicamente las actividades con los estándares básicos estatales, visita *http://www.teachercreated.com/standards.*

- Desplázate hacia abajo en la lista alfabética para encontrar la *Summertime Learning (2nd Edition)* series.
- Haz clic en **Standards** el link para acceder a TCR8843 Summertime Learning Grade 3 Standards.

Habilidades Introducidas y Reforzadas

Las actividades de *Summertime Learning: Prepare Your Child for Third Grade* tienen como objetivo reforzar las habilidades aprendidas en el segundo grado, así como introducir otras nuevas que luego serán desarrolladas en el tercer grado. Dichas habilidades se encuentran enumeradas a continuación, y en las páginas 10–11.

Habilidades de escritura

- Utiliza estrategias de escritura para diferentes propósitos y contextos
- Escribe textos informativos
- Escribe textos narrativos
- Escribe textos autobiográficos
- Escribe en respuesta a historias/obras literarias
- Utiliza el lenguaje descriptivo para ampliar ideas
- Escribe en forma de oraciones completas cuando se le indica
- Escribe en forma de párrafo cuando se le indica
- Evalúa sus producciones escritas y las de los demás
- Utiliza correctamente las diferentes partes del discurso (incluyendo sustantivos, verbos, pronombres, adjetivos, adverbios y conjunciones coordinantes) en las composiciones escritas
- Utiliza correctamente las reglas de ortografía, puntuación y mayúsculas en las composiciones escritas

Standards and Skills *(cont.)*

Habilidades Introducidas y Reforzadas *(cont.)*

Habilidades de lectura

- Realiza una vista preliminar de los textos
- Establece un propósito para la lectura
- Realiza predicciones simples sobre lo que podría hallar en un texto y las confirma/reconsidera cuando es necesario
- Utiliza claves estructurales y fonéticas para descifrar palabras desconocidas
- Utiliza claves contextuales y sintácticas para descifrar palabras desconocidas
- Comprende vocabulario de lectura acorde a su nivel
- Realiza modificaciones a sus estrategias de lectura cuando es necesario
- Ajusta la velocidad de lectura para adaptarse al propósito y al nivel de dificultad del material
- Comprende el concepto de trama
- Posee una comprensión preliminar del concepto de causa y efecto
- Establece relaciones entre los eventos de una historia y sus experiencias personales

Habilidades de Matemáticas

- Utiliza distintas estrategias para comprender los problemas
- Comprende que el modo en que se representa un problema puede ayudar en su resolución
- Utiliza la prueba y error para resolver los problemas
- Reconoce la diferencia entre información relevante y no relevante al resolver un problema
- Comprende el lenguaje básico de la lógica en contextos matemáticos
- Comprende los conceptos básicos de la teoría numérica
- Comprende formas equivalentes de porcentajes, fracciones y decimales
- Comprende el lenguaje de las operaciones básicas

Habilidades Introducidas y Reforzadas *(cont.)*

Habilidades de Matemáticas *(cont.)*

- Comprende la diferencia básica entre los números pares y los impares
- Comprende el concepto básico de valor posicional
- Comprende la relación básica entre números enteros, fracciones, decimales y números mixtos
- Utiliza modelos para identificar, ordenar y comparar números
- Multiplica y divide los números enteros de forma correcta
- Suma, resta y multiplica los decimales de forma correcta
- Suma y resta fracciones simples de forma correcta
- Utiliza estrategias para estimar cálculos
- Realiza cálculos mentales básicos
- Determina el efecto que tienen la suma, la resta, la multiplicación y la división en el tamaño y orden de los números
- Resuelve problemas del mundo real que involucran operaciones numéricas
- Escoge y utiliza las herramientas adecuadas para realizar las tareas de medición
- Utiliza estrategias específicas para estimar cantidades y medidas
- Conoce el lenguaje básico para describir y nombrar las formas geométricas
- Comprende las propiedades básicas de las figuras
- Comprende que las formas pueden ser congruentes o semejantes
- Comprende las características de las líneas y los ángulos
- Resuelve oraciones abiertas simples que involucran operaciones de números enteros
- Comprende que las ideas y conceptos matemáticos pueden representarse gráficamente

In the Shade

Directions: Fill in the missing numbers from 1–99 in the blank squares. Then, follow the directions below to shade in some of the squares.

Instrucciones: Escribe los números que faltan del 1 al 99 en los espacios en blanco. Luego, sigue las indicaciones que figuran a continuación para sombrear los cuadrados que corresponda.

0	1	2	3	4			7		
10						16			
20		22		24				28	
30			33				37		
40	41								49
50			53		55				
60	61							68	
70		72				76			
80					85				89
90	91	92	93	94		96			99

Use your pencil to shade all the squares that . . .

- have a 6 in the ones place
- are greater than 96 and less than 99
- have a 0 in the ones place
- are greater than 6 and less than 9
- have a 9 in the ones place
- are greater than 51 and less than 55
- have 64, 74, or 84 in them

After shading the squares, what word do you see? Write it in the space below.

Prefix Power

What to Know **Prefixes** are letters added to the beginning of words to change their meanings. For example, "mis–" is the prefix of the word *misunderstood.*

Directions: Look at the meanings of the prefixes below. Then, write the meaning of each word on the line. The first two have been done for you.

Instrucciones: Observa el significado de los prefijos. Luego, escribe el significado de cada una de las palabras en el renglón. Las primeras dos se encuentran dadas.

dis– = don't **pre–** = before **un–** = not

1. disobey don't obey
2. prejudge judge before
3. unhappy ____________________
4. distrust ____________________
5. unlike ____________________
6. disagree ____________________
7. unbelievable ____________________
8. pretest ____________________
9. preschool ____________________
10. dislike ____________________

Writing Numbers

Part 1 Directions: Read the words. Write the number form.

Parte 1 instrucciones: Lee las palabras. Escribe la forma numérica correspondiente.

Example: one hundred sixty-seven 167

1. seven hundred seventy-eight ________
2. four hundred thirteen ________
3. two hundred thirty-three ________
4. four hundred ninety-one ________
5. five hundred six ________
6. three hundred forty-two ________

Part 2 Directions: Write the numbers in expanded form.

Parte 2 instrucciones: Escribe los números en su forma expandida.

Example: 868 [800] + [60] + [8]

7. 765 [ ] + [ ] + [ ]
8. 557 [ ] + [ ] + [ ]
9. 186 [ ] + [ ] + [ ]
10. 914 [ ] + [ ] + [ ]
11. 225 [ ] + [ ] + [ ]
12. 701 [ ] + [ ] + [ ]

Part 3 Directions: Read the numbers. Write the word form.

Parte 3 instrucciones: Lee los números. Escribe sus formas verbales.

Example: 418 four hundred eighteen

13. 129 ________________
14. 365 ________________
15. 790 ________________
16. 661 ________________

Capital Letters

What to Know **Capital letters** are used to begin proper nouns, such as names, days, months, and titles of books and movies.

Directions: Circle the names, days, months, and titles in the sentences below. Rewrite each sentence with correct capitalization.

Instrucciones: Encierra en un círculo los nombres, días, meses y títulos en las siguientes oraciones. Reescribe cada oración usando correctamente las mayúsculas.

1. I had my birthday on a tuesday in april.

____

____

2. We will take a trip on a monday in june.

____

____

3. The first friday in october will be on the sixth.

____

____

4. Aunt lisa's favorite book is <u>charlotte's web</u>.

____

____

5. My sister wanted to read a book called <u>press here</u>.

____

____

6. The funniest character in <u>toy story 4</u> is named forky.

____

____

Number Dice

Directions: Count the dots on the dice. Record the number and the written form. The first one has been done for you.

Instrucciones: Cuenta los puntos en el dado. Registra cada número y su forma verbal. La primera respuesta se encuentra dada.

Dice	Number	Written Form
1. 	341	three hundred forty-one
2. 		
3. 		
4. 		
5. 		
6. 		
7. 		
8. 		

What was the smallest number made?

What was the largest number made?

Sequence of Events

Directions: Read the story. Then, write the events below in proper order.

Instrucciones: Lee la historia. Luego, escribe los eventos en el orden correcto.

On the night before her family vacation, Tracy began packing. She needed clothes that would keep her warm in the mountains. Tracy packed a coat and many warm sweaters. Then she packed some long pants, socks, and boots. Finally, Tracy packed some cozy pajamas. Just as she was ready to close her suitcase, she remembered her journal. She wanted to write about every detail of her vacation. As Tracy lay on her bed thinking of her exciting trip, she drifted off to sleep.

1. ______________________________

2. ______________________________

3. ______________________________

4. ______________________________

5. ______________________________

- Tracy packed her socks.
- Tracy packed her journal.
- Tracy fell asleep.
- Tracy packed her coat.
- Tracy packed her pajamas.

In Their Right Place

Directions: Look at the cans below. If the underlined digit is in the tens place, write the number in the tens-place barrel. If the underlined digit is in the hundreds place, write the number in the hundreds-place barrel. Place the ones in the ones-place barrel.

Instrucciones: Observa las latas. Si el dígito subrayado se encuentra en el lugar de las decenas, escribe el número en el barril para las decenas. Si el dígito subrayado se encuentra en el lugar de las centenas, escribe el número en el barril para las centenas. Coloca las unidades en el barril para las unidades.

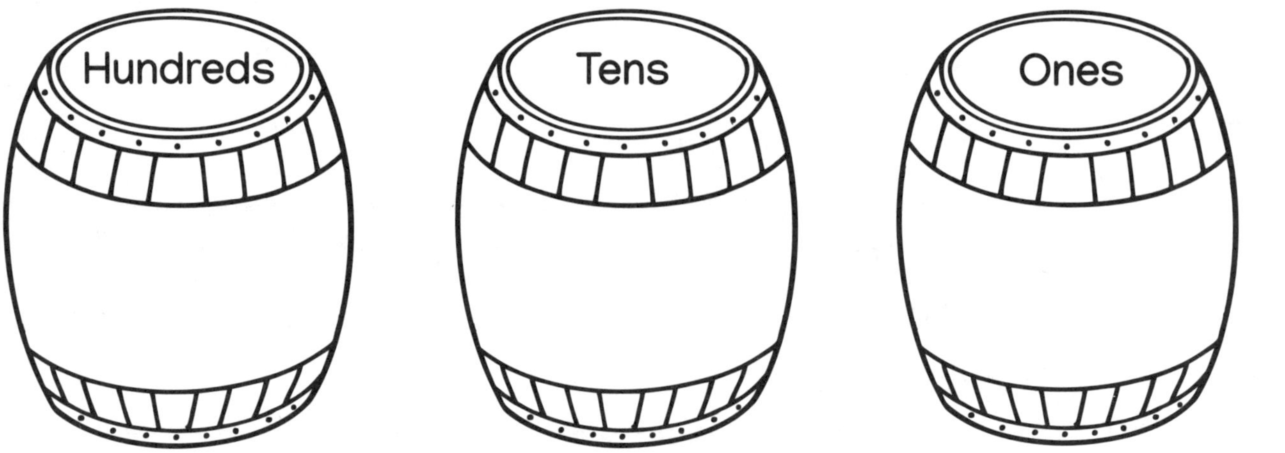

Alliteration

What to Know **Alliteration** is the use of several words close together that begin with the same consonant.

Directions: Create alliteration. Replace the underlined words with words from the Word Bank. Copy each new sentence on the line below it.

Instrucciones: Elabora aliteración. Reemplaza las palabras subrayadas por palabras del "Word Bank". Copia cada nueva oración en el renglón que se encuentra debajo.

Word Bank				
wind	berries	bear	snake	cried
silly	poured	two	breakfast	whipped
pavement	cushion	tiny	curled up	slithered

"c" words

1. The cat <u>sat</u> on the <u>pillow</u> and <u>meowed</u>.

____

"s" words

2. One Saturday, a <u>funny</u> <u>reptile</u> <u>moved</u> in the dirt.

____

"t" words

3. <u>A couple</u> <u>little</u> turtles walked to the city.

____

"w" words

4. The cold <u>breeze</u> <u>blew</u> past the lake.

____

"p" words

5. The rain <u>sprinkled</u> down on the <u>street</u>.

____

"b" words

6. The <u>animal</u> ate <u>food</u> for <u>a meal</u>.

____

Pyramid Puzzle

Directions: Alice wants to stack boxes into the shape of a pyramid. If she starts with eight blocks on the bottom and stacks one less block on each layer, how many blocks will she use to complete the pyramid? Draw the blocks on top of each row to complete the pattern. Write the total number in the top block.

Instrucciones: Alice quiere apilar las cajas para formar una pirámide. Si comienza colocando ocho bloques en la base, y apila un bloque menos en cada una de las capas, ¿cuántos bloques necesitará para completar la pirámide? Dibuja los bloques correspondientes sobre cada fila para completar el patrón. Escribe el número total en el bloque superior.

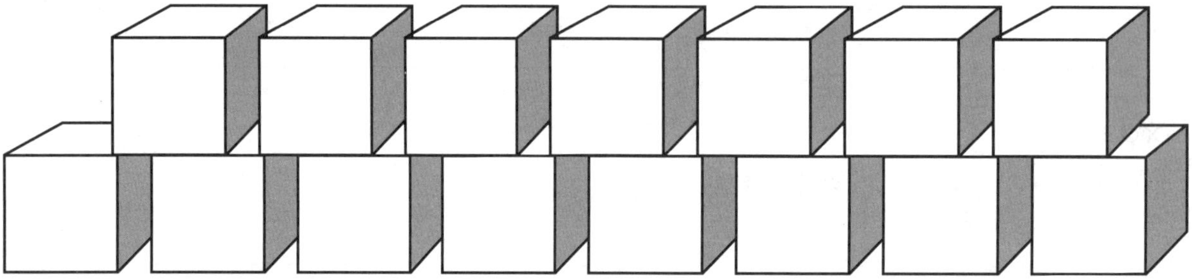

Word Searched

Directions: The words below are in the present tense. Write them in the past tense on the lines, then find them in the puzzle. The first one is done for you.

Instrucciones: Las siguientes palabras se encuentran en tiempo presente. Escríbelas en tiempo pasado sobre los renglones. Luego, encuéntralas en el crucigrama. La primera palabra se encuentra dada.

U	M	D	U	R	D	E	T	F	S	C	T	T
N	B	W	E	N	I	H	E	U	D	O	O	T
D	O	R	U	D	R	Z	R	F	W	O	F	U
E	U	O	E	E	I	P	W	E	T	K	M	V
R	F	K	W	C	R	C	N	D	S	E	T	Q
S	G	W	P	I	O	K	E	J	X	D	U	P
T	H	N	S	T	B	G	D	D	D	R	A	N
O	B	E	A	D	E	D	N	E	T	E	R	P
O	D	U	K	S	U	C	I	I	K	R	N	A
D	G	S	L	L	T	L	A	D	Z	S	G	V
H	C	L	A	P	P	E	D	U	R	E	A	N
E	V	U	Y	E	D	P	D	H	G	O	D	A
M	J	J	R	T	O	G	R	O	F	H	V	G
A	L	E	F	T	R	O	E	M	A	C	T	E

ASK ASKED

CATCH ______

CLAP ______

COME ______

COOK ______

DECIDE ______

DRIVE ______

FIND ______

FORGET ______

KNOW ______

LEAVE ______

PRETEND ______

RECOGNIZE ______

REPLY ______

SING ______

SURPRISE ______

THROW ______

UNDERSTAND ______

Add and Relax

Directions: Solve each addition problem and color the puzzle. Use the Color Code.

Instrucciones: Resuelve cada uno de los problemas de adición y colorea el dibujo. Utiliza el "Color Code".

Color Code	65 = green	66 = brown	67 = orange	68 = yellow	69 = blue

They Said It

What to Know

Use **quotation marks** around a direct quote (words being spoken). Use a **comma** to set off a quotation within a sentence. Use a **capital letter** to begin each quotation.

Directions: Place a comma and quotation marks in each sentence below. The first one has been done for you.

Instrucciones: Coloca una coma y comillas en cada una de las oraciones. La primera se encuentra dada.

1. Dr. Brown said, "You are as fit as a fiddle!"

2. Line up at the door said Mrs. Johnson.

3. Mom yelled Go, Cobras, go!

4. Sheila wondered Should I wear my blue dress?

5. My dad said You look nice today.

6. James asked May I have a glass of milk?

7. Please answer the phone whispered my mother.

8. Kelly exclaimed Look out!

9. My lizard escaped replied Henry sadly.

10. Juliette said I hope you can come over to play.

Two-Digit Addition

Example:

	tens	ones
	1	
	5	4
+	2	7
	8	1

- When adding two digits, always start on the ones side first.
- Remember, there cannot be more than 9 ones on the ones side. So take 10 of the ones, and move that set of 10 to the tens side.
- In the small square at the top of the left column (or tens column) record how many tens were moved to the tens side.
- Now, put the remaining ones under the ones column. Add the tens, and write the number.

Directions: Complete the following addition problems.

Instrucciones: Resuelve los siguientes problemas de adición.

1.

	tens	ones
	3	9
+	1	3

2.

	tens	ones
	4	2
+	2	8

3.

	tens	ones
	6	1
+	1	9

4.

	tens	ones
	2	5
+	2	5

5.

	tens	ones
	3	6
+	3	6

6.

	tens	ones
	1	8
+	1	7

Suffixes

What to Know **Suffixes** are letters added to the end of words to form new words. For example, "–less" is the suffix of the word *sugarless*.

Directions: Use the two suffix meanings below to help you figure out the meaning of each word. Write the meaning of each word on the line.

Instrucciones: Utiliza los significados de los sufijos que figuran a continuación para ayudarte a descubrir el significado de cada una de las palabras. Escríbelo en el renglón.

–ful = having a lot of **–ness** = a state of being

1. sadness being sad
2. delightful having a lot of delight
3. wonderful ______
4. careful ______
5. happiness ______
6. softness ______
7. colorful ______
8. joyful ______
9. loneliness ______
10. harmful ______

Added Challenge

Directions: Write the answer to each addition problem.

Instrucciones: Escribe la respuesta a cada problema de adición.

1.

	hundreds	tens	ones
	1	1	
	2	8	6
+	1	2	9
	4	1	5

2.

	hundreds	tens	ones
	2	9	7
+	3	0	6

3.

	hundreds	tens	ones
	4	2	5
+	1	8	8

4.

	hundreds	tens	ones
	5	0	7
+	1	2	6

5.

	hundreds	tens	ones
	8	2	7
+	1	0	3

6.

	hundreds	tens	ones
	7	2	7
+	1	7	3

Strong Verbs

Directions: Write a verb on each line. Use the words in the Word Bank to help you.

Instrucciones: Escribe un verbo en cada renglón. Utiliza las palabras del "Word Bank" para ayudarte.

Word Bank				
devoured	gazed	nibbled	stared	strolled
gasped	glanced	paced	stomped	tiptoed

1. The squirrel ______________________ on the nut.
2. The hungry lion ______________________ his food.
3. I got mad and ______________________ off.
4. Gaby ______________________ when she noticed the rattlesnake.
5. She ______________________ over her shoulder and saw the boy chasing her.
6. He ______________________ at the math problem for a long time.
7. My dad ______________________ back and forth because he was worried.
8. They ______________________ at the sunset until night fell.
9. I wanted to surprise my mom, so I ______________________ into the room.
10. The people ______________________ down the path.

They All Add Up

Directions: Arrange the numbers at the bottom of the page in the squares so that adding across in each row makes 105 and adding down in each column makes 105.

Instrucciones: Coloca los números que se encuentran al final de la página en los cuadrados, de modo que la suma de cada fila de como resultado 105, y la suma de cada columna también.

		31	This row equals 105.
	33		This row equals 105.
		39	This row equals 105.
This column equals 105.	This column equals 105.	This column equals 105.	

32	34	37
35	36	38

Who Needs That?

Directions: Read each paragraph. Find the sentence that does not fit with the rest of the sentences. Draw a line through it.

Instrucciones: Lee cada uno de los párrafos. Encuentra la oración que no concuerda con el resto. Dibuja una línea sobre ella.

1. Katie studied very hard for the spelling test. She wrote each word ten times and then tried to spell each word without looking. She was ready! She wore a red dress to school. Then the test began, but Katie got nervous. Would she remember how to spell the words?

2. It was the day of the school parade. The children were dressed in costumes. The floats were ready to go. All of the parents were gathered along the sidewalks. I can't wait for Christmas.

3. The air grew cold as the storm rolled in. The sky was cloudy and dark. Shelly's new dog ate breakfast. Thunder could be heard in the distance. Shelly decided she had better take an umbrella with her to school.

4. Planting a flower garden is easy and fun. Daisies are pretty. All you need is a plot of dirt, some seeds, and water. First, you make several small holes in the dirt. Then, you sprinkle a few seeds in each hole and cover them with dirt. Just water the garden when it's dry, and in a few weeks, your garden will begin to grow!

5. Have you ever been to a circus? I love to see all of the animals do tricks. The elephants look smart, and the dancing bears are so cute. I love to watch the man on the trapeze. That looks scary. I wonder if I can go get pizza after the show.

What's In the Box?

Directions: Find the sums. Then, write the letter in each box that matches each sum. The first one has been done for you. Read the word you spell, then draw it in the box.

Instrucciones: Resuelve las sumas. Luego, escribe en cada recuadro la letra que coincida con ese resultado. La primera respuesta se encuentra dada. Lee la palabra que formaste, luego dibújala en el recuadro.

80	81	82	83	84	85	86	87
d	e	a	o	c	r	l	i

45 + 37 = 82	17 + 67	38 + 47	58 + 25	58 + 26
a				
36 + 47	49 + 31	69 + 18	79 + 7	48 + 33

A Purple Ear

Directions: Fill in the Word Bank below, but do not look ahead at the story. Then, use the words from the Word Bank to complete your strange tale.

Instrucciones: Completa el "Word Bank" sin mirar la historia. Luego, utiliza las palabras del "Word Bank" y completa tu extraño cuento.

Word Bank

1. girl's name ______________
2. animal ______________
3. *–ing* action verb ______________
4. girl's name from #1 ______________
5. day ______________
6. time you wake up ______________
7. past tense verb ______________
8. season ______________
9. past tense verb ______________
10. bright color ______________

In a strange, mysterious jungle far, far away lived a small animal named ______________ (1). She was a(n) ______________ (2). One of her friends, Mary, had gone ______________ (3) in Rome. When she arrived home, ______________ (4) noticed that there was beautiful purple paint on Mary's left ear. She wanted her ear to look just like that, but no one sold purple paint in the jungle. Every ______________ (5) at exactly ______________ (6), she got up and looked in the mirror with great sadness. Finally, Mary promised to bring home a can of purple paint for her the next time she ______________ (7) to Rome. In the ______________ (8), Mary ______________ (9) her bags and flew to Rome! When Mary came home. the purple paint was in her hand, but her ear was ______________ (10) now!

Coin Flip

Directions: First, find a coin. Then, flip the coin.

Instrucciones: Primero, busca una moneda. Luego, hazla girar.

heads

tails

- **heads** = The problem is solved using addition.
- **tails** = The problem is solved using subtraction.

Continue flipping the coin and solving each of the problems in order. Write the sign on each problem. Good luck!

After your first coin flip, write the plus or minus sign beside problem #1. Solve problem #1. Then flip the coin to find out if problem #2 will be an addition or subtraction problem. Continue in this way until you have solved all of the problems.

1. 780 132	2. 39 15	3. 932 407
4. 555 47	5. 312 88	6. 73 47
7. 2,804 97	8. 87 49	9. 643 554

Sneaky Snake

Directions: Solve the subtraction problems. Then, fill in the number code. When you are done, read the story.

Instrucciones: Resuelve los problemas de sustracción. Luego, completa la historia utilizando el código numérico. Cuando termines, léela.

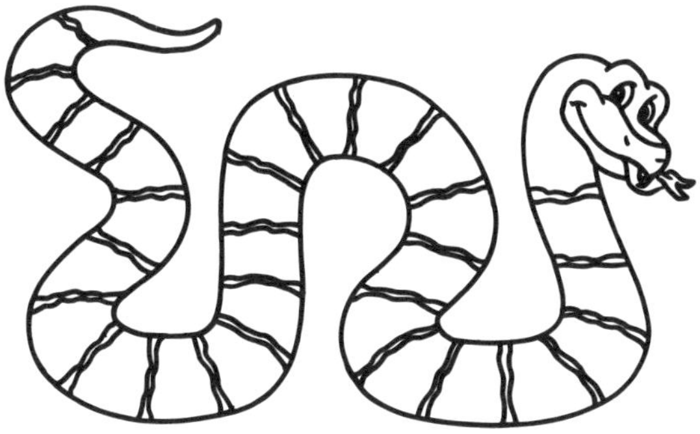

15 – 10 = ________ G	17 – 6 = ________ R
20 – 19 = ________ A	13 – 6 = ________ K
20 – 8 = ________ S	14 – 11 = ________ C
17 – 15 = ________ B	17 – 9 = ________ L
20 – 11 = ________ N	12 – 6 = ________ H
16 – 12 = ________ E	13 – 3 = ________ O

What a sneaky snake I am! I get my name from my hard, turned-up

____ ____ ____ ____. If I think someone might harm me, I flatten
9 10 12 4

my head and hiss. Then, I strike hard with my ____ ____ ____ ____,
9 10 12 4

but I don't bite. If that doesn't work, I ____ ____ ____ ____ over and
11 10 8 8

play dead! If someone picks me up, I ____ ____ ____ ____ limply.
6 1 9 5

When I'm put back down, I flip over on my ____ ____ ____ ____.
2 1 3 7

I'm a ____ ____ ____ ____ ____ ____ ____ snake.
6 10 5 9 10 12 4

I've Been Framed!

Directions: Each number below is written within a different shape or frame. Using this as a guide, write the correct number in each shape below and solve each problem. Some numbers have been written for you.

Instrucciones: Cada número que figura a continuación se encuentra escrito dentro de una forma o marco diferente. Utilizando esta información como guía, escribe el número correcto en cada una de las formas para resolver los problemas. Algunos números se encuentran dados.

8	3	5
6	9	7
4	2	1

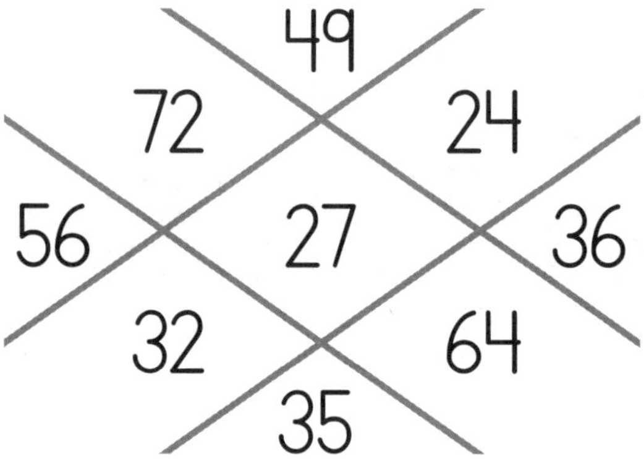

1. (35 - 5) + (27 - 3) = 54

2. (32 - ___) + (49 - ___) = ______

3. (72 - ___) + (24 - ___) = ______

4. (___ - ___) + (___ - 8) = ______

5. (___ - ___) + (35 - ___) = ______

What Do You Mean?

Part 1 Directions: Determine two meanings of each word. Use the word in different ways to write two sentences. The first one has been done for you.

Parte 1 Instrucciones: Establece dos significados para cada palabra. Utilízala de diferentes modos para escribir dos oraciones. La primera se encuentra dada.

1. hide

   Meaning #1: The puppy likes to hide under the table.

   Meaning #2: Leather is made from the hide of a cow.

2. right

   Meaning #1: ______________________

   Meaning #2: ______________________

3. left

   Meaning #1: ______________________

   Meaning #2: ______________________

Part 2 Directions: Read each sentence. Circle the correct meaning of the underlined word.

Parte 2 Instrucciones: Lee cada una de las oraciones. Encierra en un círculo el significado correcto de la palabra subrayada.

4. Be sure to <u>post</u> your message on the bulletin board.

   - a pole
   - put up

5. If I don't do a good job, the boss will <u>fire</u> me.

   - flames
   - get rid of someone from work

6. Did you already <u>pack</u> for the trip?

   - put clothes in a suitcase
   - wolves in a group

Two-Digit Subtraction

Directions: Complete the problems.

Instrucciones: Resuelve los problemas.

1.

	tens	ones
	2	0
–	1	0

2.

	tens	ones
	3	6
–	3	5

3.

	tens	ones
	3	9
–	2	7

4.

	tens	ones
	8	5
–	3	5

5.

	tens	ones
	7	8
–	4	8

6.

	tens	ones
	8	3
–	5	2

7.

	8	0
–	1	0

8.

	9	7
–	6	4

9.

	7	8
–	1	5

10. $\begin{array}{r} 25 \\ -14 \\ \hline \end{array}$

11. $\begin{array}{r} 89 \\ -41 \\ \hline \end{array}$

12. $\begin{array}{r} 91 \\ -71 \\ \hline \end{array}$

13. $\begin{array}{r} 88 \\ -28 \\ \hline \end{array}$

14. $\begin{array}{r} 94 \\ -73 \\ \hline \end{array}$

15. $\begin{array}{r} 81 \\ -61 \\ \hline \end{array}$

A Secret Story

Directions: Read the story. Then, answer the questions.

Instrucciones: Lee la historia. Luego, responde las preguntas.

Vanessa and Chloe woke up early on Saturday morning. "Mom is still asleep, I think," Vanessa whispered. "Maybe if we hurry, we can finish before she wakes up," replied Chloe. The girls tiptoed to the living room and pulled a large box from behind the couch. "Did you get the paper?" asked Vanessa. Chloe handed her the roll of bright red, yellow, and orange paper. "She's going to love this, don't you think?" Chloe smiled and said, "This will really help her in the garden." The girls finished wrapping the box and slid it behind the couch again. They heard some noises down the hallway and quickly jumped on the couch and pretended to be looking at books. "Girls," Mother said, "what are you up to?" "Nothing, Mom," they replied.

1. Who are Vanessa and Chloe? How do you know? ____________________

____

2. Why were they whispering? ____________________

____

3. What is special about this day? ____________________

____

4. How do you think Mom feels about gardening? ____________________

____

5. What do you think is inside the box? ____________________

____

Subtract & Regroup

Example:

	tens	ones
	5	
	~~6~~	[1]3
−	4	6
	1	7

- In the problem 63 − 46, the 6 ones cannot be subtracted from the 3 ones. You will need to regroup.
- Take a ten from the 6 tens. Change the 6 tens to 5, and move the borrowed ten to the ones side. Add 10 to the 3 ones. Now, there are 5 tens and 13 ones.
- Subtract the 6 ones from the 13 ones. Write the answer.
- Subtract the 4 tens from the 5 tens. Write the answer.

Directions: Complete the following subtraction problems.

Instrucciones: Resuelve los siguientes problemas de sustracción.

1.

	tens	ones
	☐	
	8	6
−	1	7
	☐	☐

2.

	tens	ones
	☐	
	6	3
−	4	5
	☐	☐

3.

	tens	ones
	☐	
	9	0
−	5	5
	☐	☐

4.

	tens	ones
	☐	
	7	1
−	5	2
	☐	☐

5.

	tens	ones
	☐	
	5	3
−	2	8
	☐	☐

6.

	tens	ones
	☐	
	4	0
−	2	9
	☐	☐

Acting Out Verbs

Directions: Look for the verbs, or action words, in each of the sentences below. Write the verb on the line. Then, act out the sentence.

Instrucciones: Busca los verbos o palabas de acción en cada una de las oraciones que se encuentran a continuación. Escribe el verbo en el renglón. Luego, actúa la oración.

1. The girl tripped over a tree branch. ____________________
2. The train rides down the track. ____________________
3. The monkey ate all the bananas. ____________________
4. The bear stood quietly in the road. ____________________
5. I scream during scary movies. ____________________
6. My teacher reads books. ____________________
7. The cat slept all day long. ____________________
8. Mark slipped on the banana peel. ____________________
9. The kids run a mile every day. ____________________
10. The dragon breathed fire. ____________________

Draw a picture of one of the sentences on this page.

Follow the Smallest

Directions: Work your way through the maze. As you come to each choice, pick the path with the smallest number.

Instrucciones: Intenta atravesar el laberinto. Al momento de decidir, escoge el camino que posea el número menor.

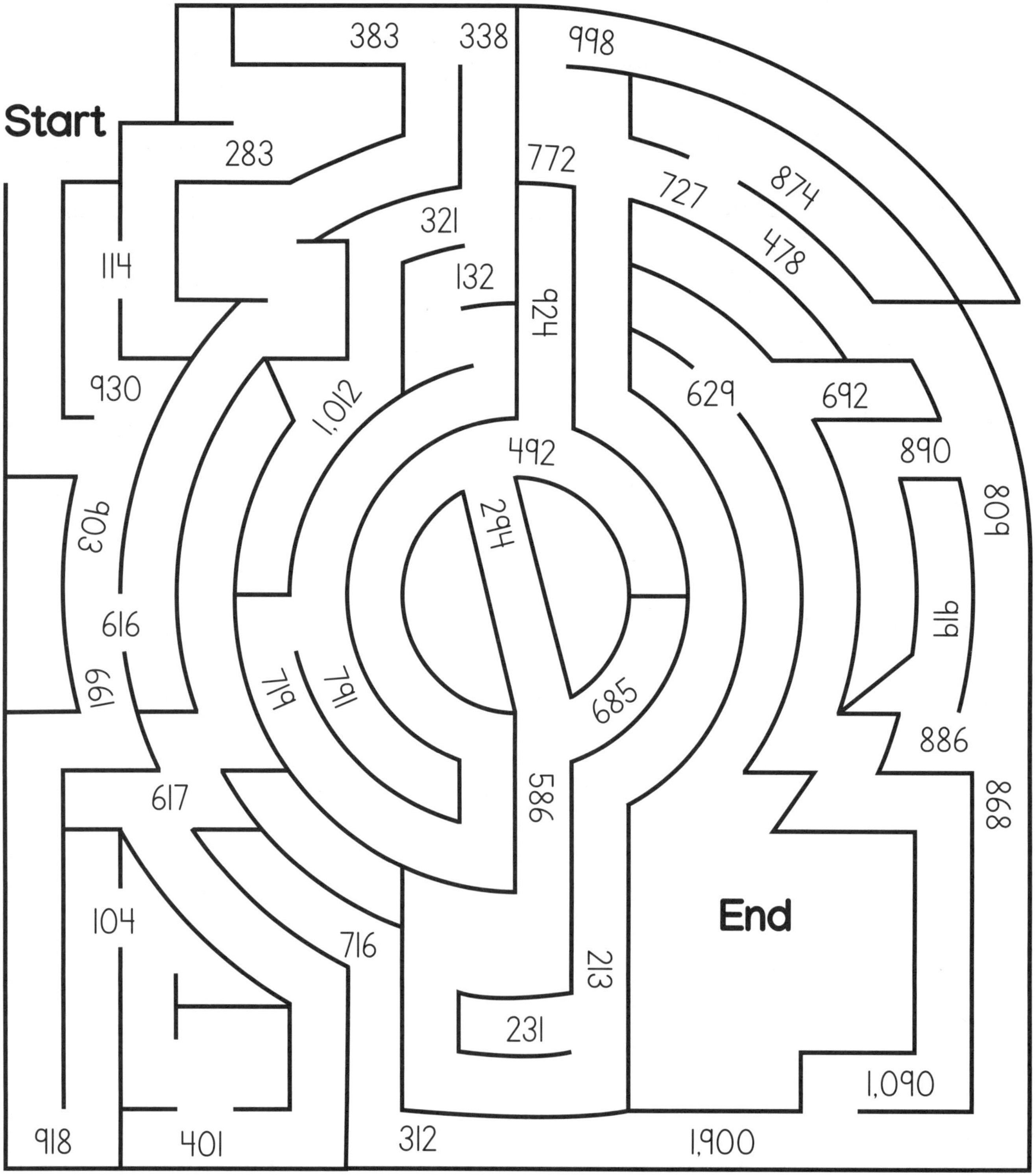

Map Madness

Directions: Do you see Jan? She is lost! Follow the map directions to get her back on track. Mark her ending spot with an **X.**

Instrucciones: ¿Puedes encontrar a Jan? ¡Se ha perdido! Sigue las indicaciones del mapa para ayudarla a encontrar su camino. Marca su punto de llegada con una **X.**

Map Directions:

1. Go west on Cat Ave.
2. Go north on Zebra St.
3. Go east on Rabbit Ave.
4. Go south on Bear St.
5. END End at the corner of Cat Ave.

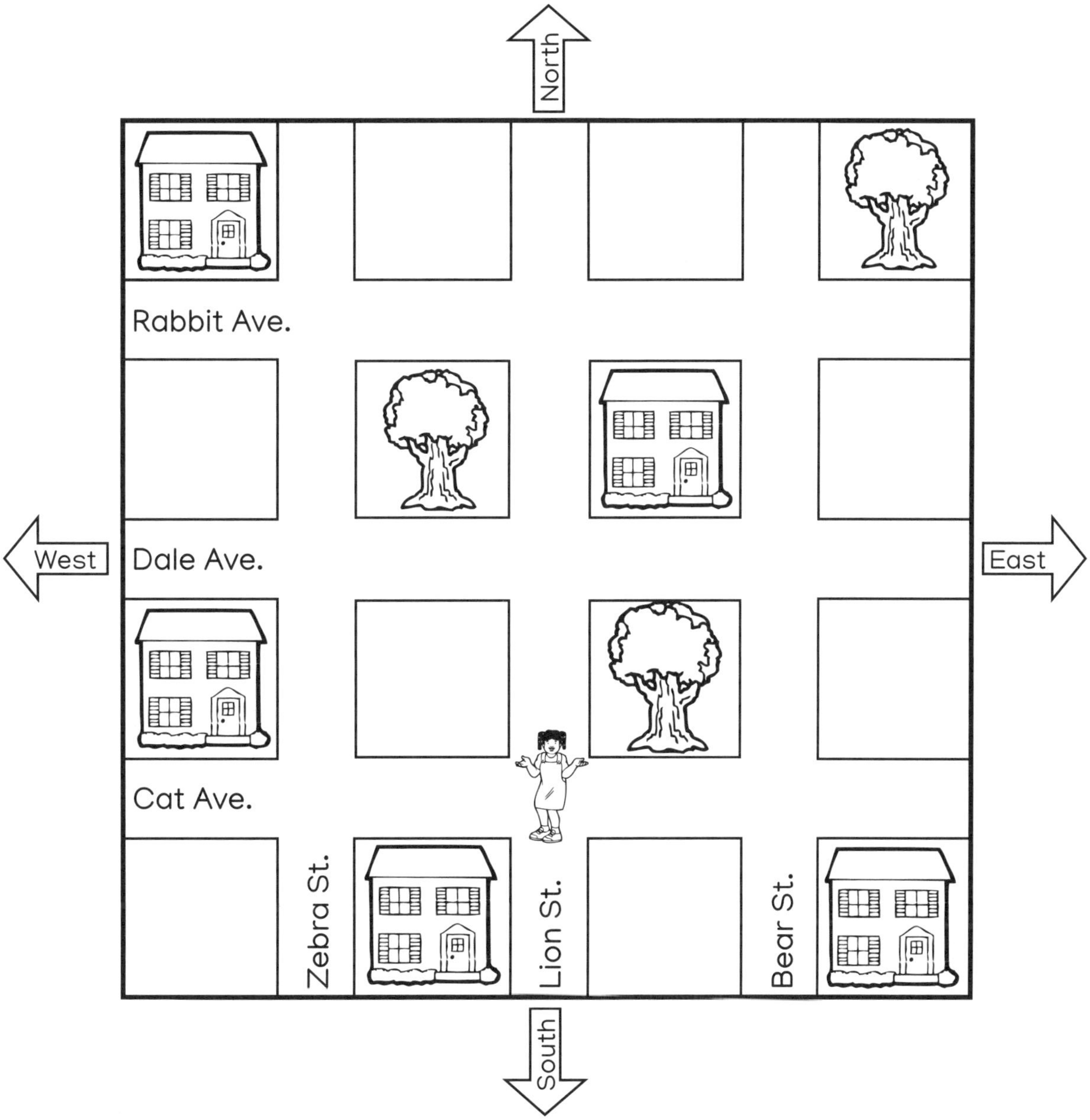

Counting Sets

Multiplication is a faster way to add sets with the same number of items.

Count and add the stars below (2 + 2 + 2 = 6 stars).

You can get the same number of stars by multiplying the number of sets times the number of items in each set (3 sets of stars × 2 stars in each set = 6 stars).

Directions: Count the number of sets and items in each set. Write the addition problem and the multiplication problem for each set of pictures.

Instrucciones: Cuenta el número de grupos y elementos en cada conjunto. Escribe el problema de adición y multiplicación para cada grupo de imágenes.

1. ____ + ____ + ____ + ____ = ________

2. ________ × ________ = ________
   (sets) (items) (product)

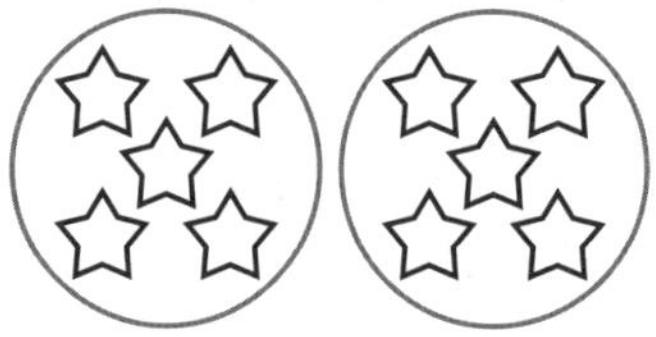

3. ________ + ________ = ________

4. ________ × ________ = ________
   (sets) (items) (product)

5. ______ + ______ + ______ = ________

6. ________ × ________ = ________
   (sets) (items) (product)

7. ___ + ___ + ___ + ___ + ___ + ___ = _____

8. ________ × ________ = ________
   (sets) (items) (product)

Describing Words

What to Know — **Adjectives** are words that tell about, or describe, nouns. Adjectives make writing more interesting.

Directions: Circle the adjective in each of the sentences below, then draw an arrow to the noun that the adjective describes. The first one has been done for you.

Instrucciones: Encierra en un círculo los adjetivos presentes en cada una de las oraciones. Luego, dibuja una flecha hacia el sustantivo que describe el adjetivo. La primera se encuentra dada.

1. The (chocolate) cake is finished.
2. The red licorice is all gone.
3. An angry man stormed out of the store.
4. Mrs. Jarski read us an interesting story.
5. David likes to write long letters to his sister.

Directions: Fill in the blanks by thinking of your own adjectives.

Instrucciones: Completa los espacios en blanco con los adjetivos que se te ocurran.

6. List three adjectives that describe you.

    __________ __________ __________

7. Write three adjectives that describe the kind of day you are having.

    __________ __________ __________

8. List three adjectives to describe your last family trip.

    __________ __________ __________

9. Write three adjectives to describe your best friend.

    __________ __________ __________

Multiplying to 100

Directions: Complete the multiplication table by filling in the missing numbers.

Instrucciones: Completa la tabla de multiplicación escribiendo los números que faltan.

×	0	1	2	3	4	5	6	7	8	9	10
0	0										0
1		1								9	
2		2	4		8				16		
3	0			9				21			
4					16		24				40
5						25	30	35	40	45	50
6					24		36	42	48	54	60
7	0			21	28		42	49	56	63	70
8			16				48	56	64	72	80
9		9					54	63	72	81	90
10	0						60	70	80	90	100

Compound Words

What to Know A **compound word** is made up of two or more words joined together.

Directions: Divide each compound word below into syllables using hyphens. The first one has been done for you.

Instrucciones: Divide cada una de las palabras compuestas en sílabas usando guiones. La primera se encuentra dada.

1. football foot-ball

2. pigpen ______________

3. snowshoe ______________

4. nighttime ______________

5. clipboard ______________

Draw a picture of one of the compound words on this page.

6. shoelace ______________

7. bedtime ______________

8. playground ______________

9. rainbow ______________

10. sunshine ______________

Twos and Threes

Directions: Complete each equation by writing the missing factor or product.

Instrucciones: Completa cada una de las operaciones escribiendo el producto o factor que le falta.

1. $2 \times 1 =$ ______	2. $2 \times 7 =$ ______	3. ______ $\times 3 = 9$
4. $2 \times$ ______ $= 2$	5. $2 \times$ ______ $= 16$	6. $3 \times 4 =$ ______
7. ______ $\times 3 = 6$	8. ______ $\times 9 = 18$	9. $3 \times$ ______ $= 15$

Directions: Answer each word problem.

Instrucciones: Resuelve cada uno de los problemas verbales.

10. Joanie has 2 marble bags. Inside each bag, there are 6 marbles. How many marbles does Joanie have in all?

    Joanie has ________ marbles in all.

11. Katie has 3 books. If she reads 10 pages in each book every day, how many pages does Katie read in a day?

    Katie reads ________ pages a day.

12. Each bin holds 2 apples. How many apples will the 8 bins hold in all?

    The 8 bins hold ________ in all.

13. Mary has 3 dogs. Each dog can eat 5 dog treats a day. How many dog treats do Mary's dogs eat in a day?

    They eat ________ dog treats a day.

Sense Sentences

Directions: A good story uses the senses to make the reader feel like he or she is really there. Try writing one sentence for each of the five senses, according to the directions below. Write so that those who read your sentences will see, hear, smell, taste, or feel what you have described.

Instrucciones: Una buena historia utiliza los sentidos para lograr que el lector sienta que realmente se encuentra allí. Intenta escribir una oración para cada uno de los cinco sentidos, siguiendo las indicaciones que figuran a continuación. Escribe de tal manera que quien lea tus oraciones pueda ver, oír, oler o sentir lo que has descripto.

1. Write a sentence that shows what the ocean **looks** like. Do not use the words *big, huge,* or *blue.*

   ____

   ____

2. Write a sentence that shows what a cat's purr **sounds** like. Do not use the words *quiet* or *low.*

   ____

   ____

3. Write a sentence that shows how a flower **smells.** Do not use the words *pretty* or *good.*

   ____

   ____

4. Write a sentence that shows what chocolate **tastes** like. Do not use the words *creamy, good,* or *sweet.*

   ____

   ____

5. Write a sentence that shows how a snake **feels.** Do not use the words *slimy* or *slithery.*

   ____

   ____

Mysterious Fives

Directions: Solve each multiplication problem. Write the letter that goes with the answer for each problem on the line at the bottom of the page. What is the question?

Instrucciones: Resuelve cada uno de los problemas de multiplicación. Escribe la letra que corresponda con la respuesta para cada uno de los problemas sobre el renglón que se encuentra al final de la hoja. ¿Cuál es la pregunta?

5	10	15	20	25	30	35	40	45	50	55
A	C	I	L	M	N	O	P	T	U	Y

1. $2 \times 5 =$ ____
2. $5 \times 1 =$ ____
3. $6 \times 5 =$ ____
4. $5 \times 11 =$ ____
5. $5 \times 7 =$ ____
6. $10 \times 5 =$ ____
7. $5 \times 5 =$ ____
8. $5 \times 10 =$ ____
9. $5 \times 4 =$ ____
10. $5 \times 9 =$ ____
11. $3 \times 5 =$ ____
12. $8 \times 5 =$ ____
13. $4 \times 5 =$ ____
14. $11 \times 5 =$ ____

___ ___ ___ ___ ___ ___ ___ ___ ___ ___ ___ ___ ___ ___ ?
1 2 3 | 4 5 6 | 7 8 9 10 11 12 13 14

On the Beach

Directions: Read the story below, then think about another way the story could have ended. What else could have happened? Write your new ending on the lines.

Instrucciones: Lee la historia que se encuentra a continuación. Luego, piensa en un final alternativo. ¿Qué mas podría haber pasado? Escribe el nuevo final en los renglones.

Carlos and Zoe often went to the beach. Carlos liked to pick up shells, and Zoe enjoyed watching the birds.

But one day, the children found something very different. Carlos saw it first because he was looking at the sand.

"Zoe," said Carlos, "Come here quickly!"

Zoe stopped watching the seagulls dive and swoop. She ran over to Carlos. He was looking at a long, brown-gray, fishy kind of animal.

"What is it?" asked Zoe.

"I think it's a small shark," said Carlos.

Zoe looked at the sharp teeth and pointy fins. She said, "I think you're right."

"Is it still alive?" asked Carlos.

"I think so," answered Zoe. "We'll have to get it in the water soon, though."

"Let's hurry home," said Carlos. "Mom and Dad can help us to safely put the shark back into the ocean."

Shoe Styles

Directions: Use the information you see in the pictures below to fill in the graph with the correct information. The "dots" column has already been filled in for you. Look at the graph, then write the answers to the questions below.

Instrucciones: Utiliza la información que muestran las imágenes para completar el gráfico con la información correcta. La columna de los "dots" ya ha sido completada. Observa el gráfico. Luego, responde las preguntas que figuran a continuación.

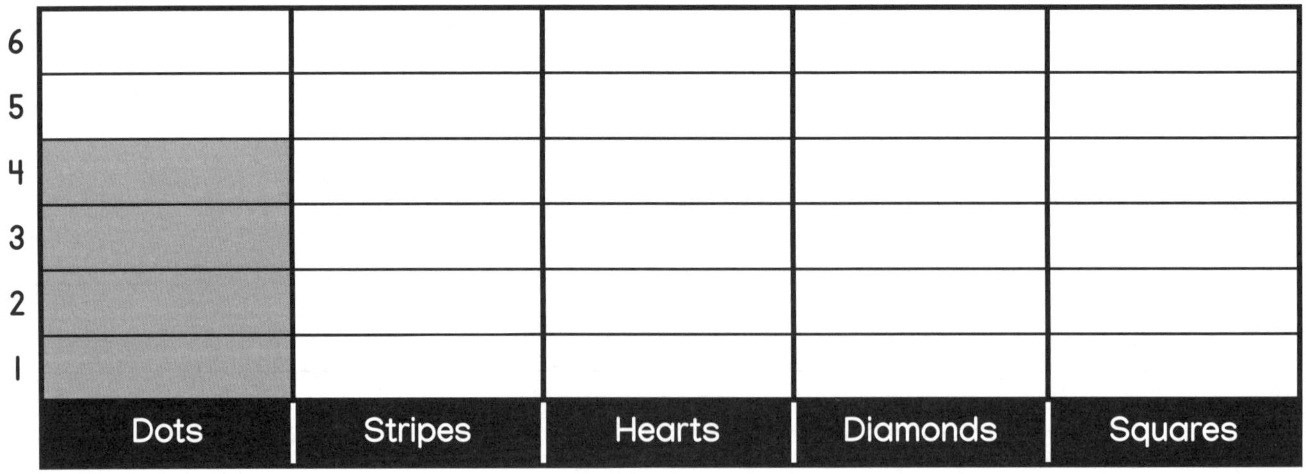

1. Which shoes did you find the most of? ____________________
2. Which shoes did you find the least of? ____________________
3. How many shoes did you find altogether? ____________________

Which Number Am I?

Directions: Read each clue. Put an X on the number(s) that do not fit each clue. After reading all of the clues, there will be one number left.

Instrucciones: Lee cada una de las pistas. Coloca una X en el/los números que no concuerda(n) con las pistas. Tras leer todas las pistas, quedará sólo un número sin marcar.

85,457	879	80,121	579
2,157	39,643	29,253	144,384
66,176	9,780	7,418	102

Clues

1. When my digits are added together, the total number is a number greater than 20 but less than 30.
2. There is one 7 in my number.
3. There are more than 3 digits in my number.
4. The number is higher than 10,000.
5. The number in the thousands place is equal to the number in the tens place.
6. Which number am I? ____________________

Subtract and Divide

It can be helpful to think of division as repeated subtraction. For example, you can use repeated subtraction to solve the following division problem.

> Jim has invented a new game using jacks. A total of 18 jacks are used to play the game. In order to play, each player must start with 3 jacks. How many people can play the game?

Think: How many 3s can I subtract from 18?

$$18 - 3 - 3 - 3 - 3 - 3 - 3 = 0$$

player 1 player 2 player 3 player 4 player 5 player 6

6 groups of 3

$$\begin{array}{r} 6 \\ 3\overline{)18} \end{array}$$

$$18 \div 3 = 6$$

Directions: Use repeated subtraction to find the answers to these problems. Show your work.

Instrucciones: Utiliza la resta repetida para hallar las respuestas a los problemas. Demuestra el trabajo realizado.

Show your work here.

1. How many 8s can you subtract from 32? ________

2. How many 5s can you subtract from 40? ________

3. How many 6s can you subtract from 24? ________

4. How many 7s can you subtract from 42? ________

Just One Sound

What to Know A **consonant digraph** is two consonants that make one sound, like /sh/ in *shop*, /ch/ in *chip*, /th/ in *that*, /wh/ in *who*, and /ck/ in *pick*.

Directions: Say the name of each picture. Circle the consonant digraph that you hear.

Instrucciones: Nombra cada una de las imágenes. Encierra en un círculo el dígrafo que has escuchado.

1.

th	wh	kn	sh	ch

2.

kn	wr	th	sh	ch

3.

kn	ch	wh	sh	th

4.

th	ch	wh	sh	kn

5.

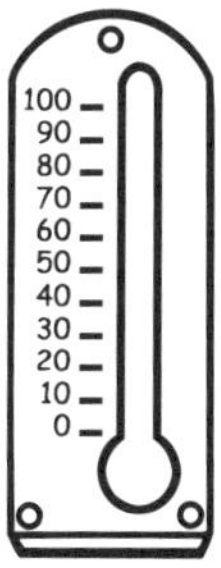

th	ch	wh	sh	kn

6.

th	ch	wh	sh	kn

7.

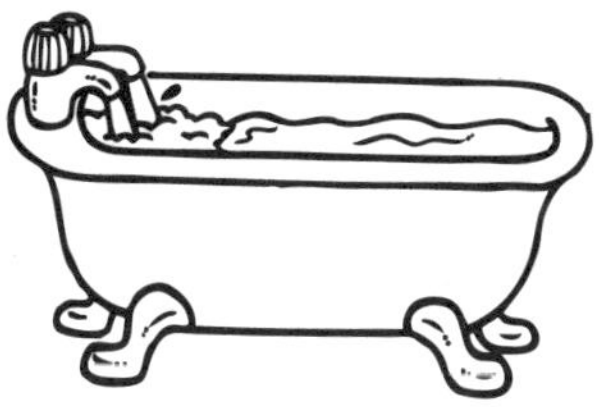

th	ch	wh	sh	kn

8.

th	wh	ch	sh	kn

9.

th	ch	wh	kn	sh

Grouping

Directions: Use different colors or patterns to make equal groups. Complete the word and number sentence to record results.

Instrucciones: Utiliza diferentes colores o patrones para crear grupos iguales. Completa las oraciones verbales y numéricas para registrar los resultados.

1. **5 in each group**

There are ______ groups of 5 hearts.

25 ÷ 5 = ________

2. **4 in each group**

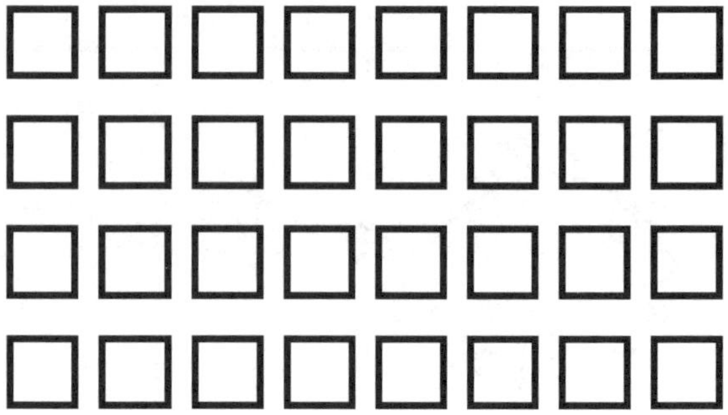

There are ______ groups of 4 squares.

32 ÷ 4 = ________

3. **3 in each group**

There are ________ groups of 3 stars.

30 ÷ 3 = ________

4. **2 in each group**

There are _____ groups of 2 triangles.

18 ÷ 2 = ________

A Series of Words

What to Know

Commas are used to separate words in a series.

Directions: Use the Word Bank at the bottom of the page to complete each sentence. Be sure to separate the words in each series with commas. The first one has been done for you.

Instrucciones: Utiliza el "Word Bank" que se encuentra al final de la hoja para completar cada oración. Asegúrate de separar las palabras de cada serie con comas. La primera respuesta se encuentra dada.

1. Would you like ___pizza___, ___pasta___, or ___steak___ for dinner?
2. The musician played __________ __________ and __________.
3. I have __________ __________ and __________ crayons.
4. I saw __________ __________ and __________ at the zoo.
5. Is this shape a __________ __________ or __________?
6. I practice on __________ __________ and __________.
7. This morning, I ate __________ __________ and __________.
8. I like to play __________ __________ and __________.

Word Bank

~~pizza pasta steak~~	lions tigers bears
bacon eggs toast	piano guitar drums
Monday Friday Sunday	red blue green
triangle square circle	soccer golf tennis

Grouping Fractions

Directions: Group, color, and count to solve each problem. The first one is done for you.

Instrucciones: Agrupa, colorea y cuenta para resolver cada uno de los problemas. La primera respuesta se encuentra dada.

1. Color $\frac{3}{4}$ of the 16 shoes. $\frac{3}{4}$ of 16 = <u>12</u> shoes.

2. Color $\frac{2}{5}$ of the 15 shoes. $\frac{2}{5}$ of 15 = ________ cookies.

3. Color $\frac{1}{2}$ of the 20 skateboards. $\frac{1}{2}$ of 20 = ________ skateboards.

High-Flying Words

What to Know

Action verbs tell what something is doing. The action verb *flying* just tells you that something is moving through the air. A different action verb can be used to show *how* that something is moving.

Directions: Read each sentence. What word would best describe how the animal is flying? Use the Word Bank to help you. Some letters have also been filled in for each answer.

Instrucciones: Lee cada una de las oraciones. ¿Qué palabra describiría mejor el vuelo del animal? Utiliza el "Word Bank" para ayudarte. Algunas letras de cada respuesta se encuentran dadas.

Word Bank			
	flapping	gliding	soaring
	fluttering	hovering	swooping

1. The eagle was going higher and higher up into the sky.

   The eagle was s o ___ r ___ n ___.

2. The butterfly was lightly bouncing from plant to plant.

   The butterfly was ___ l u ___ t ___ ___ i ___ ___.

3. The hummingbird was hanging in mid-air above the flower.

   The hummingbird was ___ o ___ e ___ i ___ ___.

4. The pelican quickly dove down to pluck a fish from the sea.

   The pelican was s ___ o o ___ ___ ___ ___.

5. The pigeon was beating its wings up and down as it flew.

   The pigeon was ___ ___ a p ___ ___ n ___.

6. The falcon stretched its wings out and let the wind move it along.

   The falcon was ___ ___ i d ___ ___ ___.

Share Evenly

Directions: Complete the problems.

Instrucciones: Resuelve los problemas.

1. You have 15 candies left in a bag. You want to divide the candy among your three friends. Draw circles showing the candies divided evenly among your friends. How many candies does each friend have? Write your answer in the box.

2. Bryson bought 20 marbles. He wants to share the marbles with his friend Jessie. Draw circles showing the marbles divided evenly between Bryson and Jessie. How many marbles does each have? Write your answer in the box.

3. Patty had 12 flowers to give to her 4 friends. Draw circles showing how Patty handed out the flowers evenly among her friends. How many flowers does each friend have? Write your answer in the box.

Sizzling Sounds

What to Know

Onomatopoeia is the use of words that sound like what they are describing, such as *buzz*, *swish*, and *growl*.

Directions: Create onomatopoeia poems. Choose a sound word from the Word Bank, then write it next to the object it describes.

Instrucciones: Completa los poemas con onomatopeyas. Escoge una palabra sonora del “Word Bank” y escríbela junto al objeto que describe.

Word Bank				
	baas	meows	pitter-patter	swoosh
	cracks	neighs	quacks	woofs

Animals

1. A cat ______________________.
2. A duck ______________________.
3. A dog ______________________.
4. A sheep ______________________.
5. A horse ______________________.

The Weather

6. The wind went ______________________.
7. The thunder ______________________.
8. The rain goes ______________________.

Brain Busters

Directions: Write the equation(s) using the correct math symbol (+, –, x, ÷) to solve each problem. The first is done for you.

Instrucciones: Escribe la(s) operación(es) utilizando el símbolo matemático correspondiente (+, –, x, ÷) para resolver cada problema. La primera respuesta se encuentra dada.

1. Number of legs on three dogs

   $3 \times 4 = 12$

   dogs

   legs on each dog

   total legs

2. Number of eyes on one person

3. Twelve eggs placed equally in three bowls

4. Number of fingers on three hands

5. How many eyes are on five three-eyed aliens?

6. Number of nickels it takes to make one quarter

7. Number of cookies in $\frac{1}{2}$ a dozen

8. There are ten points. Each star has five points. How many stars?

9. How many dimes are in one dollar?

Spell a Word

Directions: Use letters from each set to spell a word that is at least four letters long. The first answer has been given. Each problem has more than one possible answer.

Instrucciones: Utiliza letras de cada conjunto para escribir una palabra que posea por lo menos cuatro letras. La primera respuesta se encuentra dada. Cada problema posee más de una respuesta posible.

	Set of Letters	Your Word
1.	a b c d e f g	face
2.	e l a g t o f	
3.	i l m n o p s	
4.	a c e g d o m	
5.	b d f h n a e	
6.	e u t d m h s	
7.	a t g m p r e	
8.	o r s t y m a	

Writing Fractions

What to Know A **fraction** is a part (or parts) of a whole item or shape.

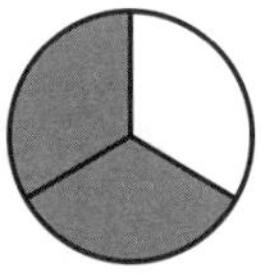

$\frac{2}{3}$

Two parts out of three are shaded.

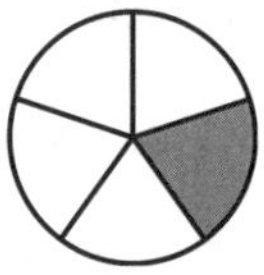

$\frac{1}{5}$

One part out of five is shaded.

Directions: Look at each shape. Write the fraction that tells how many parts of the whole object are shaded. The first one has been done for you.

Instrucciones: Observa cada una de las formas. Escribe la fracción que indique cuántas partes del objeto total han sido sombreadas. La primera se encuentra dada.

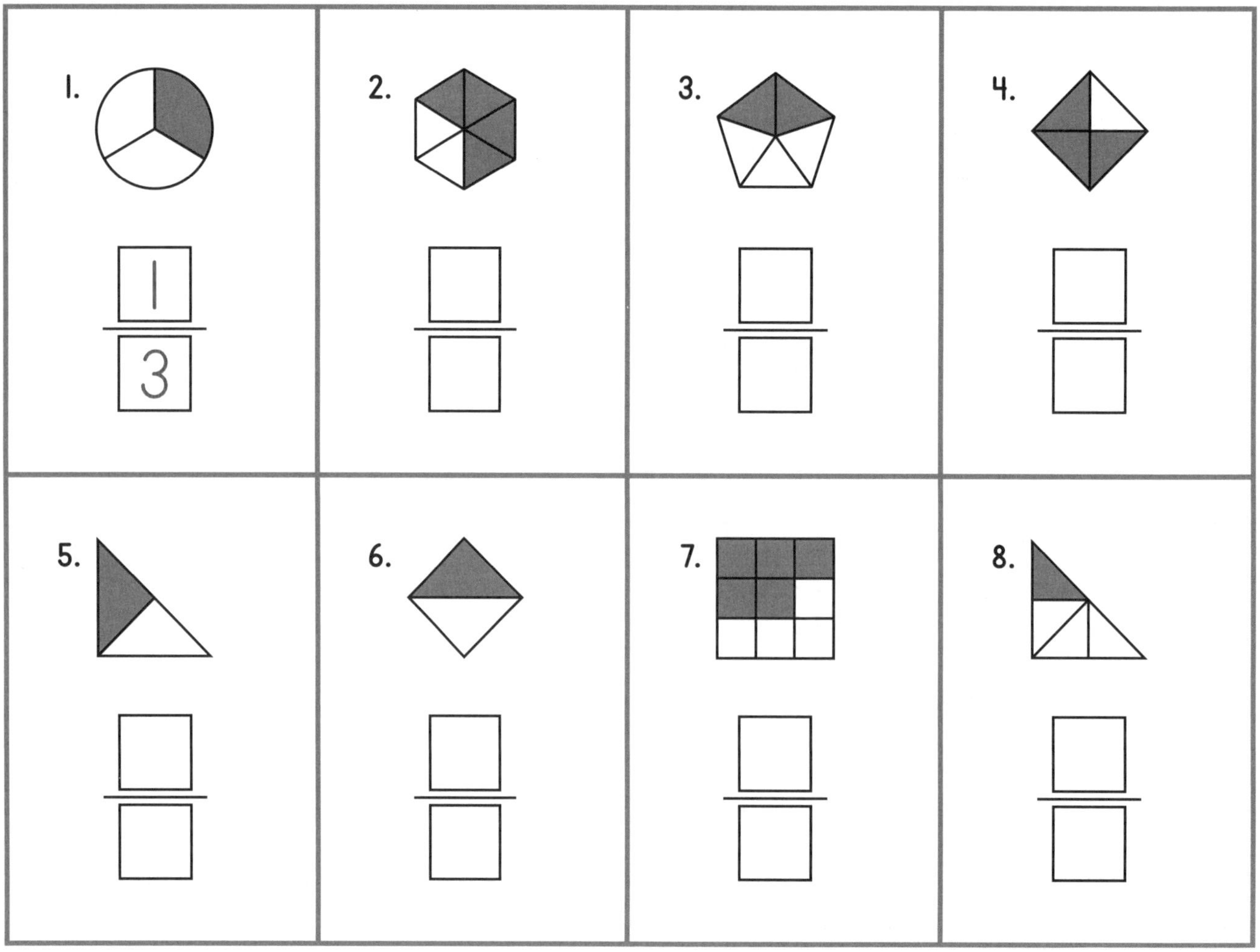

Making Sentences

What to Know

A **sentence** must make sense and must contain a subject and a verb.

Directions: For each, circle the two endings that would make sentences.

Instrucciones: En cada caso, encierra en un círculo los dos finales que podrían formar una oración.

1. The teacher
   - some white chalk.
   - told us to stand.
   - read us a story.
   - a television.

2. A large dog
   - barked at the cat.
   - with four legs.
   - chewed the bone.
   - very savage.

3. The small bird
   - built a nest in the tree.
   - on the lawn.
   - is singing a song.
   - black feathers.

Directions: Add words of your own to make sentences. The first one is done for you.

Instrucciones: Añade tus propias palabras para crear oraciones. La primera se encuentra dada.

4. dog chewed bone

   The dog chewed on the tasty bone.

5. boy lost dollar

   ____

6. truck crashed fence

   ____

Fraction Practice

Directions: Write the following fractions in standard form.

Instrucciones: Escribe las siguientes fracciones en su formato estándar.

Example: 3 out of 4 $\frac{3}{4}$

1. 6 out of 10 ________	2. 2 tenths ________
3. 5 eighths ________	4. seven-eighths ________
5. ten-twelfths ________	6. 10 out of 100 ________
7. one-half ________	8. 20 out of 100 ________

Directions: Order these fractions from smallest to largest. Remember, the larger the denominator (number under the line), the smaller each part is.

Instrucciones: Ordena las siguientes fracciones de menor a mayor. Recuerda, cuanto más grande el denominador (el número que se encuentra bajo la línea), más pequeña cada parte.

9. $\frac{1}{3}, \frac{1}{10}, \frac{1}{4}$ ________	10. $\frac{3}{10}, \frac{5}{10}, \frac{8}{10}$ ________
11. $\frac{2}{4}, \frac{2}{5}, \frac{2}{3}$ ________	12. $\frac{1}{8}, \frac{7}{8}, \frac{3}{8}$ ________
13. $2, 1\frac{1}{2}, 4\frac{1}{2}$ ________	14. $\frac{1}{5}, \frac{1}{6}, \frac{1}{2}$ ________

Synonyms

What to Know Synonyms are words that are the same or almost the same in meaning. For example, *large* is a synonym for *big*.

Directions: Each problem has two sentences. Start by finding a word in the Word Bank that would make sense in the top sentence. Write that word. Then, complete the next sentence with a synonym of that word. The first answer has been written for you.

Instrucciones: Cada problema se compone de dos oraciones. Comienza buscando una palabra en el "Word Bank" que daría sentido a la primera oración y escríbela. Luego, completa la siguiente oración con un sinónimo de dicha palabra. La primera respuesta se encuentra dada.

Word Bank					
baby	chilly	friends	infant	quietly	silently
~~buddies~~	cold	gift	present	shop	store

1. The two girls have been best ______buddies______ since preschool.

   The two girls have been best ____________ since preschool.

2. The laughing ____________ crawled toward the toy.

   The laughing ____________ crawled toward the toy.

3. Everyone in the library read their books ____________.

   Everyone in the library read their books ____________.

4. We will buy him a fun game at the toy ____________.

   We will buy him a fun game at the toy ____________.

5. I am going to wrap this ____________ in blue paper.

   I am going to wrap this ____________ in blue paper.

6. The winter weather in the mountains is often very ____________.

   The winter weather in the mountains is often very ____________.

Name That Fraction

Directions: Name the fraction that is shaded. The first answer is given.

Instrucciones: Nombra la fracción sombreada. La primera respuesta se encuentra dada.

1. 

   $\frac{2}{4}$

2. 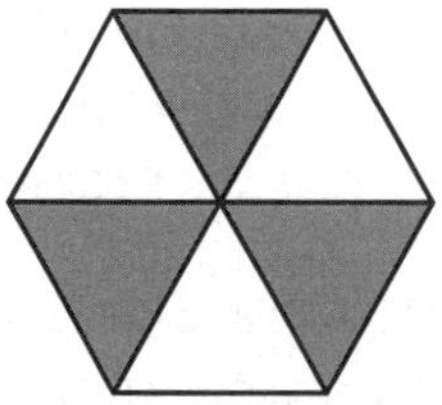

   ______

3. 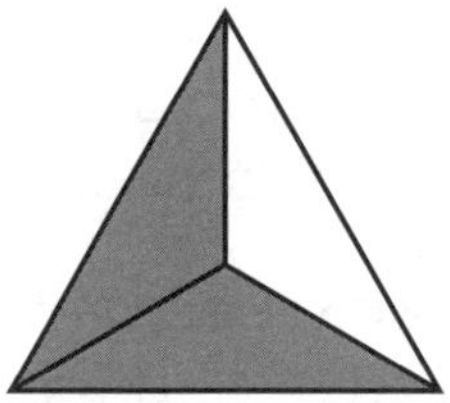

   ______

4. 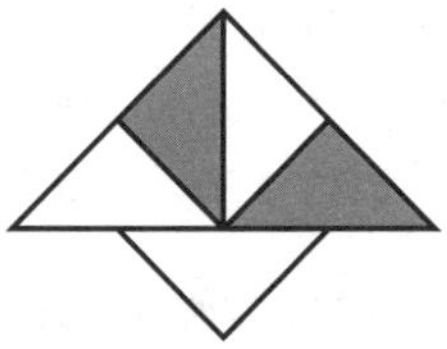

   ______

5. 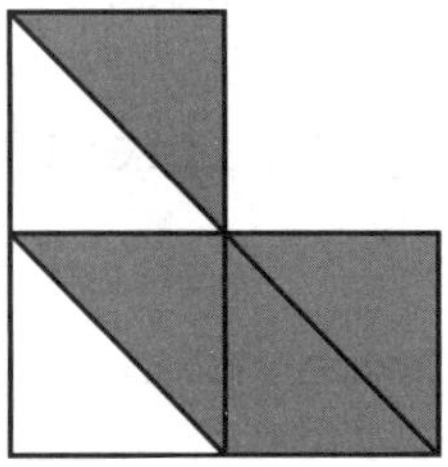

   ______

6. 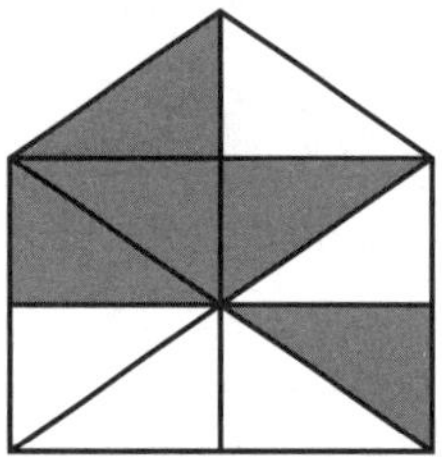

   ______

7. 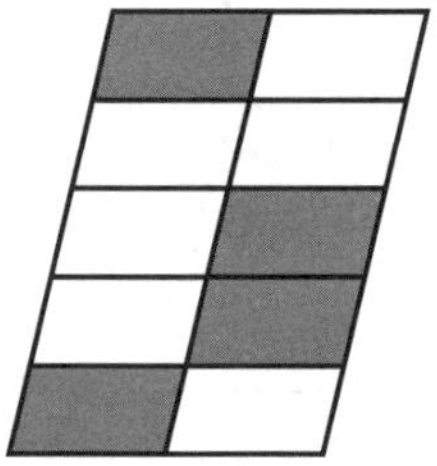

   ______

8. 

   ______

9. 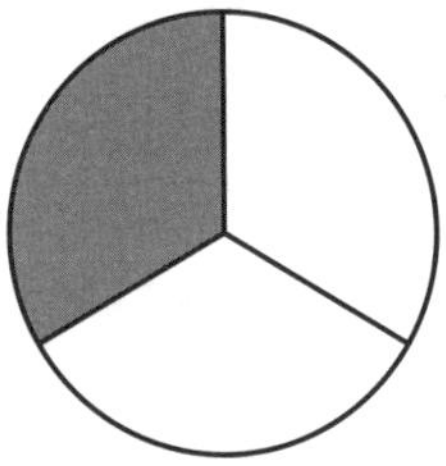

   ______

10. 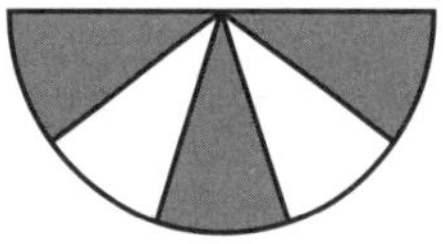

    ______

11. 

    ______

12. 

    ______

Show, Don't Tell

What to Know Good writing doesn't tell; it shows. It gives details that help readers form pictures in their minds.

Directions: First, circle the sentences below that let you "see" or "feel" what is described. Underline the sentences that just tell you about it. Next, rewrite the sentences you underlined. The first two have been done for you.

Instrucciones: Primero, encierra en un círculo las oraciones que te permitan "ver" o "sentir" lo que se describe. Subraya las oraciones que sólo te lo informan. Luego, reescribe las oraciones que subrayaste. Las primeras dos se encuentran dadas.

1. There was a tall, blue vase full of bright purple daisies on the oval table.
2. Ms. Hill is nice.
3. Maria saw a tiny, white dog, with muddy paws and a nervous tail.
4. I live in a house.
5. The shiny penny shone in the sun as it lay on the dull, gray road.
6. That's a noisy car.

Rewrite sentences here.

2. Ms. Hill shared her giant bag of candy corn with all of us.

A Fair Share

What to Know A **fraction** is a part of something. Most things can be divided into smaller or equal parts.

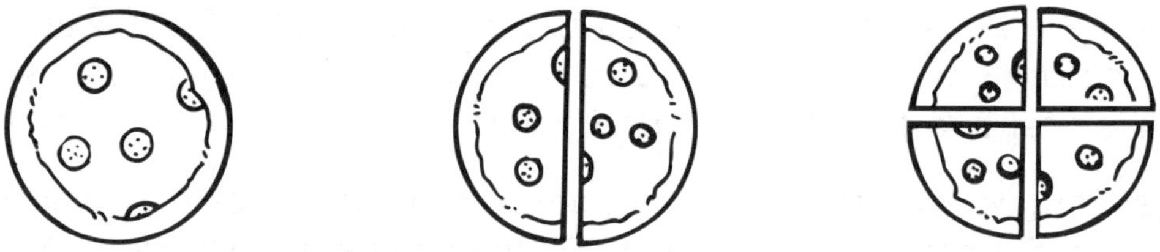

Directions: Follow the instructions below.

Instrucciones: Sigue las indicaciones que figuran a continuación.

1. Draw a circle around the picture that shows the fraction $\frac{1}{2}$.
2. Place an X on the picture that shows the fraction $\frac{1}{4}$.
3. Divide the circle into two equal parts.
4. Divide the square into four equal parts.
5. Divide the rectangle into three equal parts.

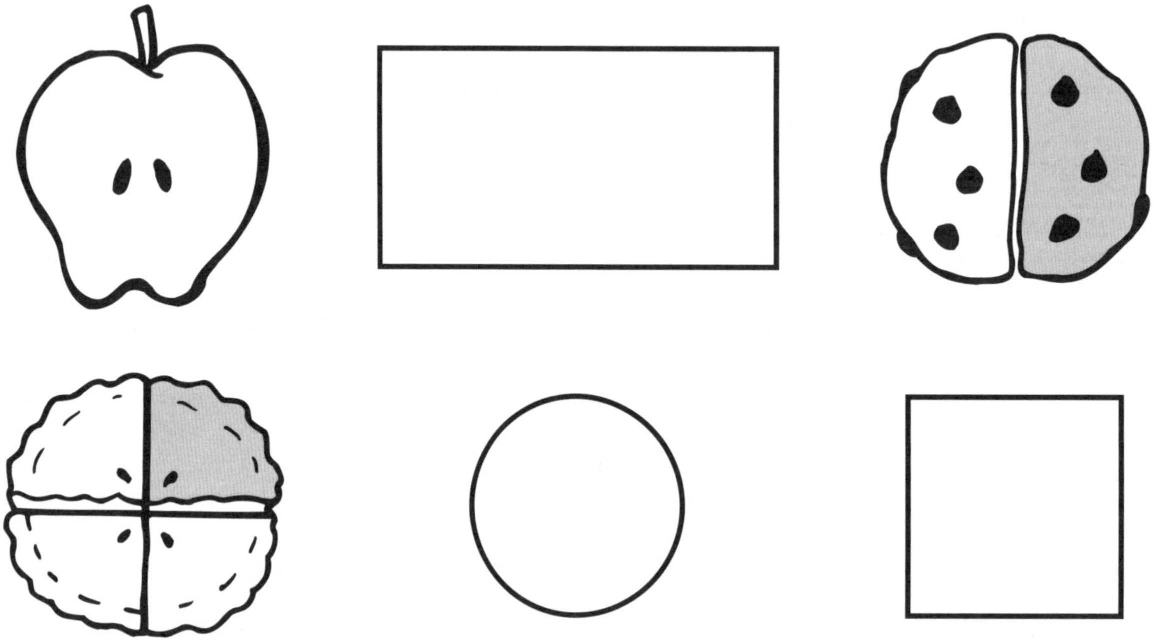

What To Call It?

Directions: Read the story. Then, complete the web below by writing a title for the story in the center oval and the main events in the surrounding oval.

Instrucciones: Lee la historia. Luego, completa la red que figura a continuación escribiendo un título para la historia en el óvalo central y los eventos principales en los óvalos que lo rodean.

Farmer Grey woke up as the sun was rising. He had a lot of work to do. So he went to the barn and gave fresh hay to the horses. He cleaned the pigpen and fed the chickens. He checked the hen house and collected the eggs from the nests. He ran inside and put the eggs in the refrigerator. Then, he hiked out to the pasture to check on the cows. After that, Farmer Grey headed back to the house. He opened the door and smelled eggs and bacon cooking in the kitchen. All that work, and the day had only just begun!

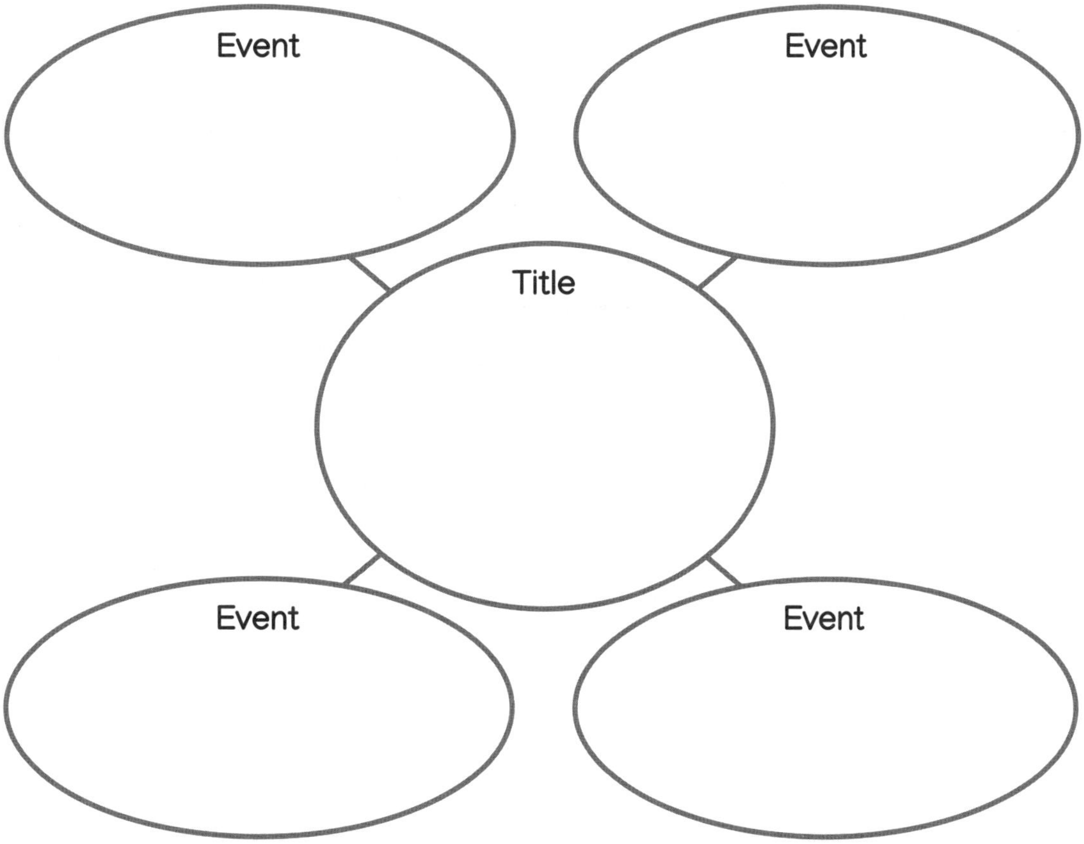

Fraction Art

Directions: Identify the fraction. Then, color the puzzle. Use the Color Key.

Instrucciones: Identifica cada una de las fracciones. Luego, colorea el dibujo. Utiliza el "Color Key".

Color Key	halves = red	thirds = blue	fourths = yellow	fifths = green

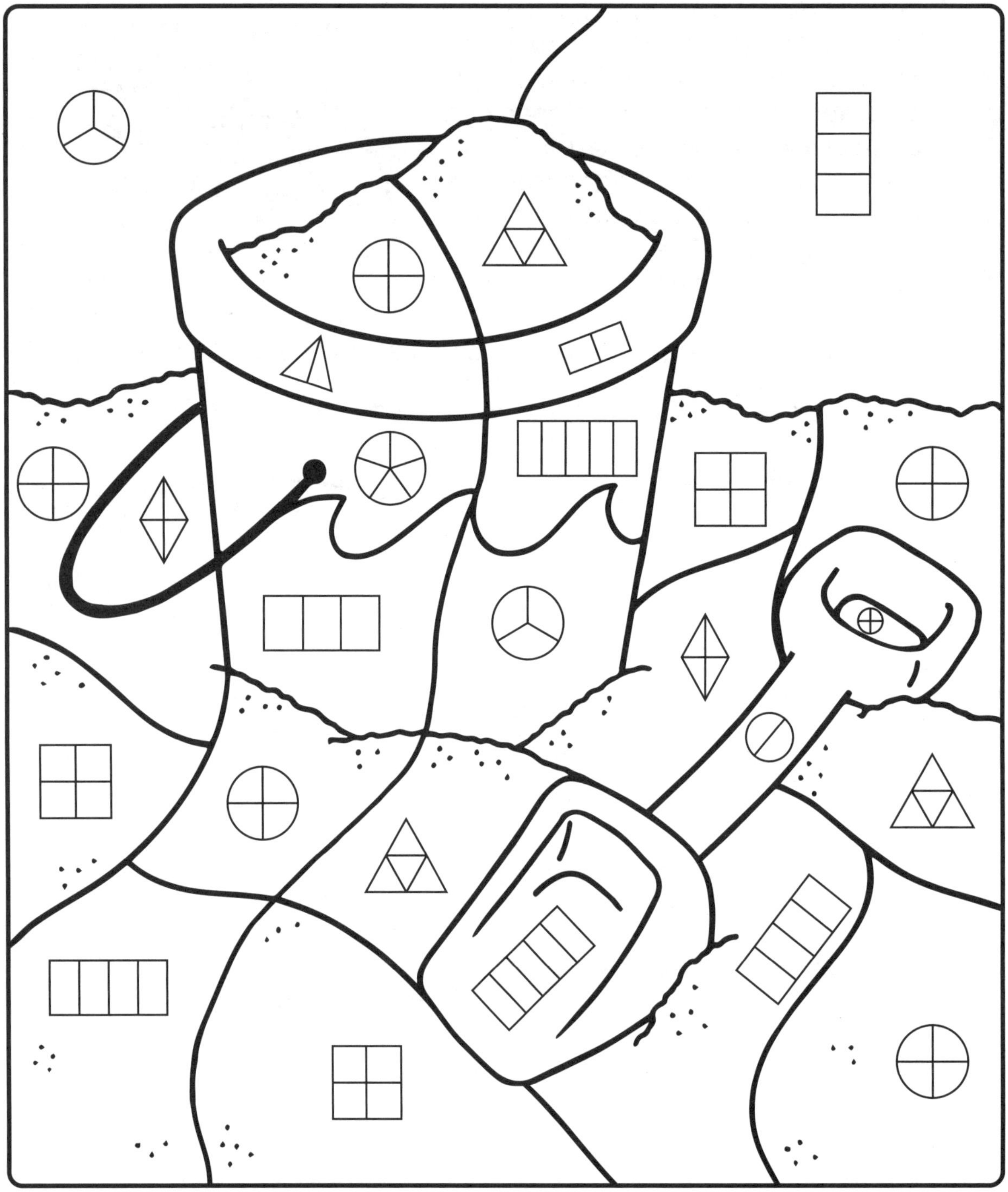

Time for Bed

Directions: It's time for bed. Find and circle these two-word bedtime actions. But look carefully! Each word in each two-word action is only connected by one letter. An example is done for you.

Instrucciones: Es hora de ir a la cama. Encuentra y encierra en un círculo las siguientes acciones relacionadas con la hora de dormir. ¡Observa con atención! Cada una de las palabras que componen las acciones se encuentran conectadas por una letra. Observa el ejemplo que se ofrece a continuación.

Actions to Find

BRUSH TEETH	~~READ STORY~~	CLOSE EYES
TAKE BATH	UNDER COVERS	FALL ASLEEP
WEAR PAJAMAS	LIGHTS OUT	

S	W	L	E	E	W	S	T	O	R	Y
T	D	I	R	E	E	A	F	M	E	S
S	W	G	E	P	A	J	A	M	A	S
E	T	H	S	U	R	B	L	D	D	R
O	U	T	T	S	A	S	L	E	E	P
E	N	S	E	E	A	M	S	T	S	W
E	D	Y	E	T	E	D	B	A	T	H
R	E	S	O	L	C	T	E	K	A	M
S	R	E	V	O	C	S	S	E	W	E

Bonus Directions: Which letters in the top two rows of the puzzle are **not circled**? Write them in order. What do they say?

Word Problems

Steps to Solving Word Problems

1. **Read** the word problem a few times.
2. **Underline** the words that give you facts or clues about whether to add, subtract, multiply, or divide.
3. **Draw** a picture to show the solution, or use real items to solve the problem.
4. **Write** the math sentence, and solve the problem.

Directions: Draw a picture and write out the math sentence to solve each word problem below. The first one has been started for you.

Instrucciones: Realiza un dibujo y escribe la oración numérica correspondiente para resolver cada uno de los problemas verbales. La primera respuesta se encuentra iniciada.

1. Robert has three marbles in each bag. He has two bags. How many marbles does Robert have in all?

$2 \times 3 =$

or

$3 + 3 =$

2. Jackie had 19 footballs. His friends borrowed 8 of the footballs. How many does Jackie have left?

3. The Tigers scored the following points: 9, 7, 5, 3, and 7. What was the sum of their points?

4. Susie has 21 tennis balls. She would like to give them to her friends so each one has the same number of tennis balls. She has 7 friends. How many can she give to each friend?

Antonyms

What to Know

Antonyms are words that are opposite or almost opposite in meaning. For example, *up* is an antonym of *down*.

Directions: Find a word in the Word Bank that means the opposite of each picture below. Print the word on the line.

Instrucciones: Encuentra una palabra del "Word Bank" que posea el significado opuesto de lo que se observa en cada imagen. Escríbela en el renglón.

Word Bank	awake	day	down	dry	empty	go

1.

____

2.

____

3.

____

4.

____

5.

____

6.

____

Number Sentences

Directions: Read each word problem. Write the number sentence. Then, find the answer.

Instrucciones: Lee cada uno de los problemas verbales. Escribe la oración numérica. Luego, resuélvelo.

1. At the circus, Kenny saw 16 tigers and 27 monkeys. How many animals did he see in all?

_______ + _______ = _________

2. When Lyla went to the tidepools, she counted 28 seastars and 46 shells. How many things did she see in all?

_______ + _______ = _________

3. Jason bought a pair of shoes for $53. Clark bought a pair for $28. What is the difference paid?

_______ – _______ = _________

4. Jill counted 83 ants near an anthill. Jack counted 65. What is the difference in the ants counted?

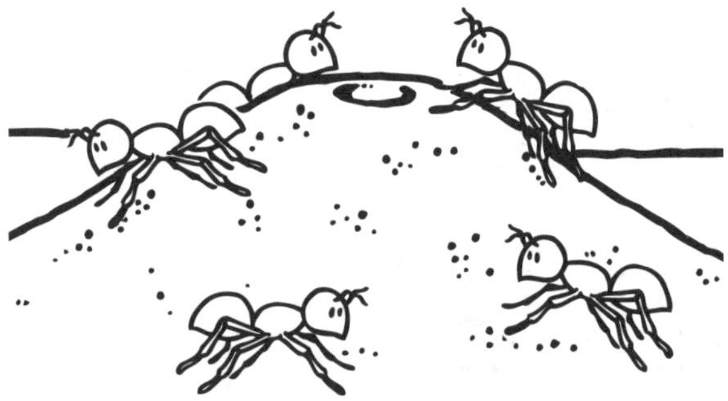

_______ – _______ = _________

Amazing Adverbs

What to Know — **Adverbs** are words that tell about, or describe, verbs.

Examples: The horse ran *quickly.*

I walked *quietly.*

The author wrote *well.*

Directions: Write the adverb that describes the underlined verb in each sentence.

Instrucciones: Escribe el adverbio que describa al verbo subrayado en cada oración.

1. Anne and Tom work hard. ____________________
2. Elise and Erica ate quickly. ____________________
3. Ethan listens intently. ____________________
4. The horse ran fast. ____________________
5. Cows eat grass slowly. ____________________
6. Mrs. Smith yelled loudly. ____________________

Directions: Write an adverb to describe each verb.

Instrucciones: Escribe un adverbio que describa cada uno de los verbos.

7. jumped ____________________	8. flew ____________________
9. skipped ____________________	10. slept ____________________

Your Own Words

Directions: Read the following word problems. In your own words, then write down what you need to find out. Then, solve each problem.

Instrucciones: Lee los siguientes problemas verbales. Con tus propias palabras, escribe lo que tienes que averiguar. Luego, resuelve cada uno de los problemas.

1. Your best friend has a bag with 203 marbles. You have 164 marbles in your backpack. How many marbles do you and your friend have altogether?

   I have to find out ______________________________

   ______________________________.

Solution: ____________

2. You have a bag with 25 candies in it. Sarah has a jumbo jar with 5 times as many candies in it. How many candies does Sarah have?

   I have to find out ______________________________

   ______________________________.

Solution: ____________

3. Your little sister has 30 dimes in her piggy bank. How many dollar bills could she get for those 30 dimes?

   I have to find out ______________________________

   ______________________________.

Solution: ____________

4. A baseball mitt costs $18.89. You have saved $9.40. How much more money do you need to buy the mitt?

   I have to find out ______________________________

   ______________________________.

Solution: ____________

Read a Recipe

Directions: Read the information in the box. Answer the questions that follow. Circle the letter beside the best answer.

Instrucciones: Lee la información presente en el recuadro. Responde las preguntas. Encierra en un círculo la letra que se encuentra junto a la mejor respuesta.

Here is a great recipe for a hot day. You will need:

- dishpan or cookie sheet
- 2 tbsp. dish soap
- warm water
- wire hangers

1. Fill the dishpan or cookie sheet with warm water and dish soap, and mix well.
2. Make bubble wands by bending each wire hanger into any shape you like. You could make a circle, an oval, or even a diamond. Straighten the hooked end into a handle.
3. Dip your wand into the bubble mixture and wave it around in the air. You should have giant bubbles!

1. According to the story, making giant bubbles is a good thing to do
   - a. during the summer.
   - b. at a dress-up party.
   - c. during recess.
   - d. during the winter.
2. What is the second step in the instructions?
   - a. Make a bubble wand out of a hanger.
   - b. Wash the dishpan or cookie sheet.
   - c. Dip the wand into the bubble mixture.
   - d. Fill a dishpan or cookie sheet with warm water.
3. How many different things will you need to make giant bubbles?
   - a. seven
   - b. six
   - c. four
   - d. three
4. The best way to answer the question right before this one is to
   - a. guess the number of things you will need.
   - b. imagine that you are making the bubbles.
   - c. count the number of things on the "you will need" list.
   - d. count the number of steps in the instructions.

Key Words

Directions: Underline the key word(s) in each problem. Solve the problem, then write the answer in the box. The first one has been done for you.

Instrucciones: Subraya la(s) palabra(s) clave(s) en cada problema. Resuelve el problema. Luego, escribe la respuesta en el recuadro. La primera respuesta se encuentra dada.

1. Rosie took 12 pictures of her cat and 15 pictures of her dog. How many pictures altogether did Rosie take of her animals?

$$\begin{array}{r} 12 \\ +\ 15 \\ \hline 27 \end{array}$$

27 pictures

2. There were 8 monkeys in the tree and 4 monkeys on the log. How many more monkeys were in the tree than on the log?

3. Mom bought 30 large plastic cups and 15 small plastic cups for the party. How many total cups did Mom buy?

4. The library had a summer reading contest. The girls read 139 books, and the boys read 128 books. What is the sum of the books the boys and girls read this summer?

5. Mrs. Simmons bought 50 pencils at the store. She gave 26 of the pencils to her students. How many pencils does Mrs. Simmons have left?

6. The gardener planted 44 flowers in the first row and 40 flowers in the second row. What is the difference between the number of flowers in the two rows?

Synonym Story

Directions: Write a synonym above each underlined word. Use a thesaurus if needed. Then, copy the story on the lines below.

Instrucciones: Escribe un sinónimo sobre cada palabra subrayada. Utiliza un diccionario de sinónimos en caso de ser necesario. Luego, copia la historia en los renglones.

One day, a father and his child left their house.

They walked to the park. They wanted to play.

They ran through the grass and laughed. Then

they saw birds in the trees. A pretty butterfly

floated by. It was a great day.

Sun Sudoku

Directions: Fill every square with an indicated color. No color can be repeated in a column, row, or box.

Instrucciones: Rellena cada cuadrado con el color indicado. No se deben repetir colores en la misma columna, fila o recuadro.

R = Red	Y = Yellow	B = Blue
O = Orange	G = Green	P = Purple

O		Y		P	B
	P		G	Y	
P		R		G	
	Y	O			P
	O	G		B	
	R				G

Compound Crossword

Directions: Complete each clue below with a compound word. Use the Word Bank to help you.

Instrucciones: Completa cada una de las pistas con una palabra compuesta. Utiliza el "Word Bank" para ayudarte.

Word Bank

- butterfly
- cupboard
- doorbell
- grandmother
- grasshoppers
- lipstick
- mailbox
- newspaper
- raincoat
- tablecloth

Across

1. My mom told me to drop the letters in the ______________.
8. Before Sandra put out the plates, she put on the ______________.
9. Steven opened the ______________ and found it was empty.
10. Annette put on her mother's ______________.

Down

2. A ___________ was once a caterpillar.
3. My ______ spent a week at our house.
4. My dad likes to read the ___________ every morning.
5. Maria liked watching the ___________ jump on her lawn.
6. Bob had to wear his ___________ every day this week.
7. Karen rang the neighbor's ___________ three times.

Rounding Numbers

Directions: Solve each word problem by rounding each number to the nearest ten and then adding or subtracting. Show your work in the space provided. The first one has been done for you.

Instrucciones: Resuelve los problemas verbales redondeando cada número a la decena más cercana y luego realizando una suma o una resta. Demuestra el trabajo realizado en el espacio provisto. La primera respuesta se encuentra dada.

1. Jason invited 39 girls and 22 boys to his party. About how many children did Jason invite in all? The number 39 is rounded to 40. The number 22 is rounded to 20. About ___60___ children were invited to the party.	40 + 20 60
2. Mariah bought 152 balloons, 127 party hats, and 213 candles for the party. About how many party items did Mariah buy in all? Mariah bought about ________ party items in all.	
3. Beau sent out 185 invitations. Eighty-seven people said "yes." The rest said "no." About how many people said "no?" About________ people said "no."	
4. Lucy set out 210 green jellybeans, 315 red jellybeans, and 57 orange ones. About how many jellybeans did Lucy set out in all? Lucy set out about ________ jellybeans.	
5. Sprinkles were put on 3 cupcakes. The children used 567 sprinkles in all. The first cupcake had 237 sprinkles. The second cupcake had 197. About how many sprinkles did the third cupcake have? The third cupcake had about ________ sprinkles.	
6. Darts were played at the party. Ben scored 222 points. Jacob scored 303 points. Elena scored 368 points. About how many points were scored in all? About ________ points were scored in all.	

Twice as Nice

Directions: Add adjectives, or describing words, in the spaces below. Then, draw pictures to match your descriptions.

Instrucciones: Añade adjetivos o palabras descriptivas en los espacios que figuran a continuación. Luego, realiza dibujos que coincidan con tus descripciones.

a ______________ ______________ apple	a ______________ ______________ house
a ______________ ______________ pencil	a ______________ ______________ tree
a ______________ ______________ monster	a ______________ ______________ vacation

Math Snacks

Directions: Read the Snack Bar Menu. Then, read the word problems. First, estimate how much each order will cost. Then, compute the total cost.

Instrucciones: Lee el "Snack Bar Menu". Luego, lee los problemas verbales. Primero, estima cuánto costará cada orden. Luego, calcula el monto total.

Snack Bar Menu

SANDWICHES		DRINKS		SNACKS	
hamburger	$1.12	soda	$0.75	chips	$0.60
cheeseburger	$1.46	juice	$0.64	apple	$0.38
fish	$1.24	water	$0.52	pretzels	$0.22
chicken	$1.39	milk	$0.48	popcorn	$0.56
peanut butter	$0.98			candy	$0.43

1. DeMarco was very hungry. He ordered one cheeseburger, one bag of chips, one apple, and a bottle of water. What was his total cost?

   Estimate: ____________________ Answer: ____________________

2. Dion only wanted snacks and a drink. He ordered one bag of pretzels, one bag of popcorn, and a can of soda. What was his total cost?

   Estimate: ____________________ Answer: ____________________

3. David decided he was hungry, too, so he ordered one fish sandwich, two boxes of candy, and one bottle of water. What was his total cost?

   Estimate: ____________________ Answer: ____________________

4. Boyd and Terrell were hungry after working at the Snack Bar. They bought one hamburger, one chicken sandwich, two cans of soda, one container of milk, two bags of popcorn, and one box of candy. What was their total cost?

   Estimate: ____________________ Answer: ____________________

The Perfect Drink

Directions: Read the information in the box. Then, follow the directions to answer the questions below.

Instrucciones: Lee la información presente en el recuadro. Luego, sigue las indicaciones para responder las preguntas.

All About Water

You could say that water is nature's perfect drink. It helps your body do so many things. Water carries oxygen to all of the cells of your body. It helps you use the food you eat. It helps you sweat when you run and play, and it helps you get better when you are ill. This is why you need extra water when you are sick and when you exercise. Your body is working harder, and water helps it do that.

Water is not just in your glass. Many foods that you eat have a lot of water in them. Think of juicy fruits, like peaches and oranges. Vegetables are full of water, too.

Do you know what else is full of water? You! Over half of your body's weight comes from water. It's *that* important.

1. All of these people need water. Circle the two who need the most water right now.

2. Some of these foods have the a lot of water in them. Circle the two that have the most.

3. How much water do you drink each day? Do you think you get enough? Should you drink more? Write two sentences about you and water.

Solving Problems

Directions: Solve each problem. Show your work.

Instrucciones: Resuelve cada uno de los problemas. Demuestra el trabajo realizado.

1. I had a whole pie. I cut it in half. How many pieces of pie do I have now?

I have ____________ piece(s) of pie.

2. Rocky ordered a pizza. The pizza was cut into four equal pieces. Rocky ate half of the pizza. How many pieces did Rocky eat?

Rocky ate _______ piece(s) of pizza.

3. Ricky had nine marbles. He kept $\frac{1}{3}$. He gave $\frac{1}{3}$ to Sonya and $\frac{1}{3}$ to Len. How many marbles does each person have now?

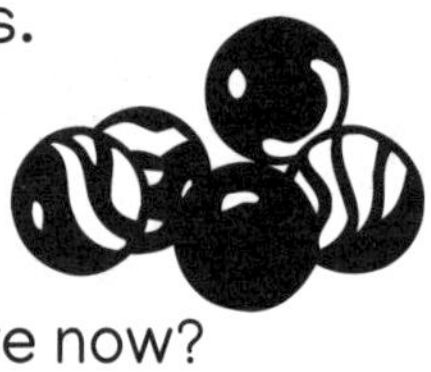

Each person has ______ marble(s).

4. Marilyn had five houses. She sold $\frac{1}{5}$ of them. How many houses did she keep?

Marilyn kept ____________ house(s).

Breakfast Box

Directions: Draw more donuts in the box. Then, describe each kind of donut. Tell what they taste like or what makes them special.

Instrucciones: Dibuja más donas en la caja. Luego, describe cada tipo. Cuenta cómo crees que sabe o qué la hace especial.

Draw 3 more donuts here.

Draw 3 more donuts here.

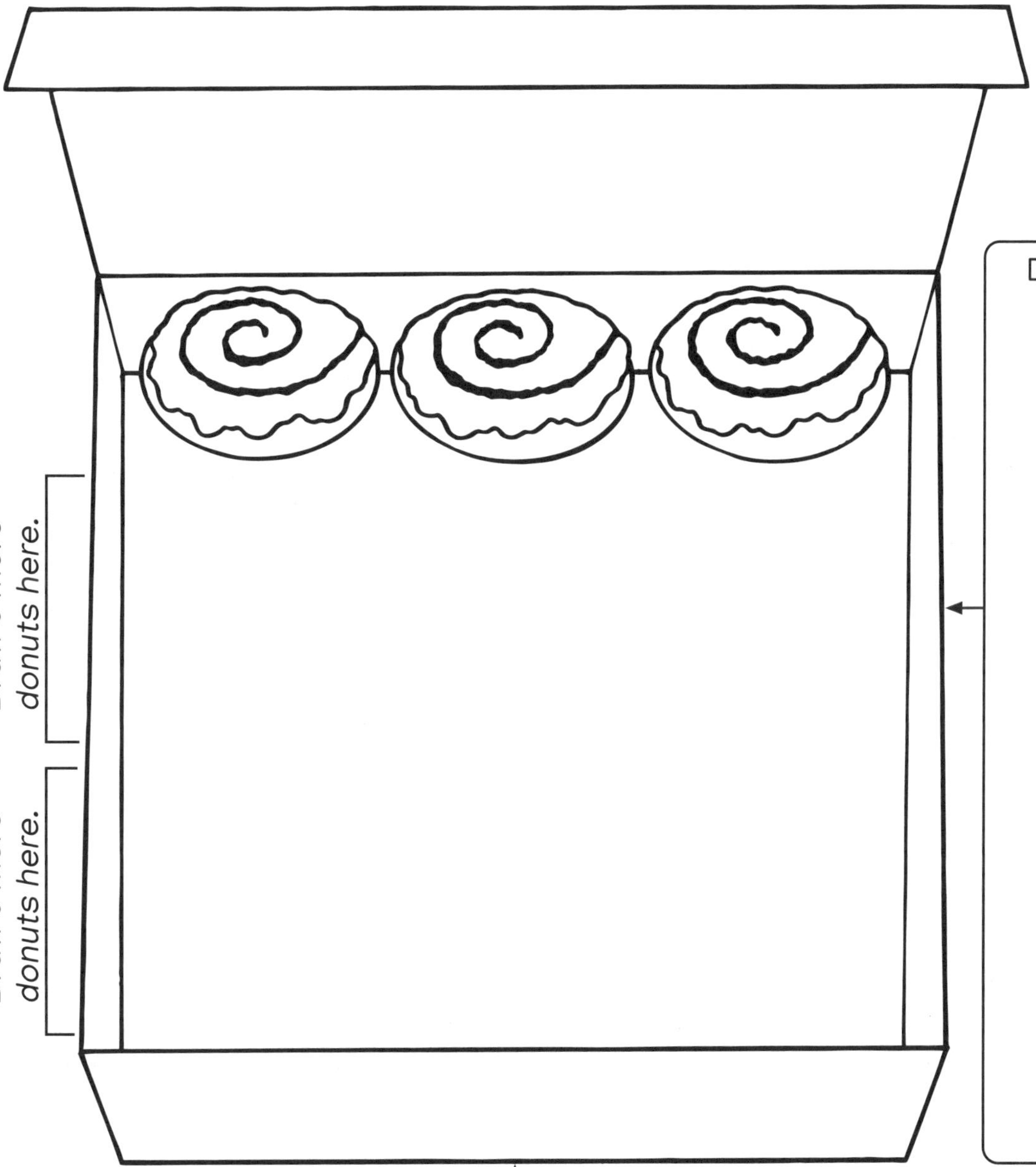

Describe here.

Describe here.

Money Madness

Directions: Solve each money riddle.

Instrucciones: Resuelve cada uno de los acertijos de dinero.

1. Michelle has five coins in her pocket. Together the coins equal 47¢. What coins does Michelle have in her pocket?	2. Kevin has three coins in his pocket. The coins are all of the same value. The coins equal 75¢. What coins does Kevin have in his pocket?
3. Matt has four coins in his pocket. The coins are all of different values. The coins equal 41¢. What coins does Matt have in his pocket?	4. Corinne has two coins in her pocket. The coins are of the same value and equal $1.00. What coins does Corinne have in her pocket?
5. Riley has six coins of three different values. Together, the coins equal 80¢. What coins does Riley have in her pocket?	6. Brandon has seven coins in his pocket. Together, the coins equal 51¢. What coins does Brandon have in his pocket?

Using Schedules

What to Know

Schedules play an important part in our lives. We have schedules for each day at school. We have schedules for sports days and swim meets. From a schedule, you can work out how long things take.

Directions: This schedule shows what Luke's class does on a Friday. Read it, then answer the questions below.

Instrucciones: El siguiente cronograma muestra lo que hace la clase de Luke durante los viernes. Léelo y luego responde las preguntas.

Schedule—Friday	
Time	**Subject**
9:00 a.m.	Weekly assembly—Room 3C
9:30 a.m.	Story writing
10:15 a.m.	Math
10:45 a.m.	SNACK
11:00 a.m.	RECESS
11:20 a.m.	Art
12:20 p.m.	Computers with Ms. Grey
12:45 p.m.	LUNCH
1:30 p.m.	Quiet reading time
2:00 p.m.	Science
2:30 p.m.	P.E. with Mr. Castle
3:10 p.m.	End of classes

1. What time does Luke start school? ____________________
2. How long is recess? ________________________ minutes
3. Which lesson is the longest? ______________________________
4. Who teaches P.E. to Luke's class? ______________________________
5. When does math finish? ____________________
6. What does the class do at 1:30 p.m.? ______________________________

Starts with CH

Directions: Find and circle 15 words that begin with the letters "ch." Find words going across, down, backwards, and diagonally.

Instrucciones: Encuentra y encierra en un círculo 15 palabras que comiencen con las letras "ch". Pueden hallarse de forma horizontal, vertical, invertida y diagonal.

Word Bank		
CHALK	CHEF	CHIMPANZEE
CHAPTER	CHERRY	CHOOSE
CHEAP	CHICKEN	CHOP
CHECK	CHILD	CHUNK
CHEESE	CHIRP	CHURCH

A	C	H	I	L	D	C	H	I	R	P
C	O	C	L	E	C	H	E	A	P	V
H	H	H	H	M	E	A	K	C	C	C
U	E	E	Z	N	A	P	M	I	H	C
R	C	F	E	M	N	T	H	E	I	K
C	H	O	O	S	E	E	R	T	C	R
H	A	H	A	H	E	R	E	E	K	Y
O	L	E	C	F	Y	S	H	C	E	O
O	K	P	O	H	C	C	H	U	N	K

Bonus Directions: Which is the only circled word in the puzzle that doesn't begin with the /ch/ sound as in "chat" or "chin"?

____

Sundae Fun Day

Directions: Each picture has something in common with the other pictures in its row and column. Find the thing that makes each row the same. Fill in your answers at the bottom of the page. The first answer is given for you.

Instrucciones: Cada una de las imágenes posee algo en común con las demás presentes en su fila y columna. Descubre lo que tiene en común cada fila. Escribe tus respuestas al final de la página. La primera se encuentra dada.

Row 1 Across: chocolate sauce on the left scoop

Row 2 Across: ______________________

Row 3 Across: ______________________

Column 1 Down: ______________________

Column 2 Down: ______________________

Column 3 Down: ______________________

Summer Reading List

Uno de los mejores modos de promover el desarrollo educativo durante el verano es mediante la lectura. Afortunadamente, existe una gran variedad de fantásticos libros ilustrados y de pasta dura que podrían interesas y cautivar a tu joven lector. Por favor, lee las reseñas y/o lee los libros tú mismo antes de presentárselos a tu hijo, con el fin de determinar si son adecuados para él.

Si lo deseas, puedes utilizar este gráfico (y el que figura en la página 93) para mantenerte organizado. Utiliza la columna de **Dates** para anotar el día en que tu hijo leyó el libro o cuándo debería devolverlo en la biblioteca. Utiliza la columna de **Notes** como ayuda para recordar lo que has leído en las reseñas de otros lectores o lo que tu hijo pensó del libro tras leerlo.

Dates	Book Information	Notes
	Ghost of the Southern Belle: A Sea Tale by Odds Bodkin Captain LeNoir's ship may have crashed on rocks and sank, but he and his ghostly crew continue to haunt the waters where they met their demise.	
	A Boy Called Slow by Joseph Bruchac This true story of Sitting Bull tells the coming-of-age tale of a great warrior who stayed true to himself and chose his own path in life, even when he was not understood by those around him.	
	Keeper of the Doves by Betsy Byars Four sisters tease and torment an old man who once saved their father's life as they learn about loyalty and life.	
	Granny Torelli Makes Soup by Sharon Creech Granny Torelli imparts life lessons and advice to her granddaughter while making and sharing Italian food.	
	The Lemonade War by Jacqueline Davies Not only is Evan's little sister skipping third grade, but she's also going to be in Evan's fourth-grade classroom at the beginning of the year! This starts a war to see which of them can make the most money in the week before school starts.	
	The Miraculous Journey of Edward Tulane by Kate DeCamillo This is an enchanting and enriching story about the journey of Edward Tulane, a toy rabbit made entirely of fine china, as he goes from living a life of luxury to finding true friendships and love in circumstances he never imagined.	
	The Gollywhopper Games by Jody Feldman The Golly Toy & Game Company's Ultimate Championship is the only thing standing between Gil Goodson and true happiness. Can he beat the other kids on live TV?	
	Sir Reginald's Logbook by Matt Hammill Sir Reginald writes about his search for the mysterious "Lost Tablet of Illusion." Is it in the deepest jungle? Is it on the tallest peak? Or is it some place more familiar?	
	How Strong Is It? by Ben Hillman This is a nonfiction book that compares the strength of twenty-two different objects or animals, including glue, gravity, and spider webs.	
	Babymouse #9: Monster Mash by Jennifer L. Holm and Matthew Holm This graphic novel will surely capture your attention! Babymouse wants to have the best Halloween party and the best Halloween costume. But she runs into some obstacles along the way.	

Summer Reading List *(cont.)*

Dates	Book Information	Notes
	Dragon Keepers #1: Dragon in the Sock Drawer by Kate Klimo Jesse finds a "thunder egg" while out hunting for rocks one afternoon. Soon, something is asking to be let out of the egg... and the adventure begins!	
	Savvy by Ingrid Law Mib, who is almost a teenager, is in a magical family when disaster strikes her Poppa. She only hopes her magical power, which hasn't blossomed yet, can save him!	
	Long Shot: Never Too Small to Dream Big by Chris Paul This picture book full of action-packed illustrations and descriptive text tells the story of a real-life NBA star who had to work hard and dream big in order to overcome others' ideas about who he was and what he was capable of accomplishing.	
	Dog Man by Dav Pilkey This wild and inventive graphic novel about a detective who is part dog and part human is beloved by many kids but not always by their parents. Be aware that this book contains a lot of potty humor and may not be appropriate for your family. However, it is also a book that has gotten a lot of reluctant readers to stick with it from cover to cover and to become more excited by the prospect of reading.	
	Pictures of Hollis Woods by Patricia Reilly Giff Hollis, an orphan, has always wished for a family and one day is adopted by a retired art teacher for whom she becomes a caregiver.	
	Sideways Stories from Wayside School by Louis Sachar Wayside School was built wrong; it should have thirty classrooms side by side, but they were built on top of each other instead! This collection of short stories introduces you to the students and staff of Wayside School—characters you'll never forget!	
	Where I Live by Eileen Spinelli Told in a series of easy-to-read poems, this is a touching tale about a family forced to move from their beloved home when the father loses his job. Will they ever feel comfortable in their new home?	
	Piper Reed, Navy Brat by Kimberly Willis Holt Piper Reed's father is in the Navy and has already moved her family around more times than she can count. Will she and her sisters survive the latest move to Pensacola, Florida?	

Aprovechando al máximo la lectura de verano

Cuando leas estos libros con tu hijo, puedes hacerle las preguntas que aparecen a continuación. El intercambio de preguntas, respuestas e ideas incrementará y potenciará sus habilidades de comprensión lectora. Estimúlalo a explayarse en sus respuestas y explicar sus pensamientos en detalle.

- ¿La portada del libro te pr ovoca deseos de abrirlo y leerlo?
- ¿De qué trata la historia?
- ¿Adónde transcurre la historia? ¿Te gustaría visitar ese sitio?
- Nombra un personaje de la historia que te haya gustado. ¿Por qué te gustó ese personaje?
- Nombra un conflicto presente en la historia. ¿Cómo se resolvió?
- Si puedes, busca una imagen que represente con exactitud lo que cuentan las palabras de la historia. Luego, busca una que represente algo que no haya sido contado en la misma.
- ¿Recomendarías este libro a tus amigos? ¿Por qué sí o por qué no?

Read and Do

A continuación, se incluyen algunas ideas divertidas para que tu hijo incremente su lectura. La mayoría implicarán la participación de ambos, pero se encuentran dirigidas hacia él con el fin de incentivar su amor por los libros.

Design a Bookmark __/__/__	You can design a bookmark for your favorite book, and then use it in other books to remind you of a great reading experience. Use a strip of colorful paper and include the title, the author, and a picture of something that happened in the book.
Write to the Author __/__/__	Many authors love to hear from their readers, especially when they hear what people liked best about their books. You can write to an author and send your letter in care of the book's publisher. The publisher's address is listed directly after the title page. Or you may go to the author's website and follow the directions for how to send the author a letter. (To make sure your author is still living, do a search on the Internet, typing the author's name into a search engine.)
A Comic Book __/__/__	Turn your favorite book into a comic book. Fold at least two sheets of paper in half, and staple them so they make a book. With a ruler and pencil, draw boxes across each page to look like blank comic strips. Then, draw the story of your book as if it were a comic. Draw pictures of your characters, and have words coming out of their mouths—just as in a real comic strip.
Always Take a Book __/__/__	Maybe you've had to wait with your parents in line at the post office or in the vet's waiting room with nothing to do. If you get into the habit of bringing a book with you wherever you go, you'll always have something exciting to do! Train yourself to always take a good book. You might want to carry a small backpack or shoulder bag—something that allows you to carry a book easily from place to place. Don't forget a bookmark!
Learn a New Skill __/__/__	What skills are mentioned in your favorite book? Perhaps a character learns to ride a unicycle. Other characters may create beautiful pottery, learn to juggle, take black-and-white photographs, train dogs, or bake five-layer cakes. Identify a skill mentioned in your book. Gather together the materials you'll need to learn this skill. Keep in mind that learning a new skill may take several weeks or months. Commit to practicing this skill at least twice a week. Keep a journal detailing your growing abilities. Finally, organize a talent show to demonstrate your newfound skill!

Read-Together Chart

Does your father read books to you before bed? Perhaps your mother reads to the family at breakfast? Your grandparents may enjoy reading books to you after school or on the weekends. You and your family members can create a Read-Together Chart and fill it in to keep track of all the books you've read together.

Here are two Read-Together Charts. The first one is a sample. The second one has been left blank, so you can add your own categories and books.

Book We Read	Who Read It?	What It's About	Our Review
Charlotte's Web	My dad read it to me.	It's about a special pig who is saved first by a girl and then by a kind spider.	Great book! I loved rooting for Wilbur. I never thought I could like a spider until I met Charlotte!

This page may be reproduced as many times as needed.

Learning Experiences

A continuación, se incluyen algunas actividades divertidas y de bajo costo que puedes realizar junto a tu hijo. Pronto descubrirás que las mismas pueden ser estimulantes, educativas y complementarias del resto de los ejercicios del libro.

Tarjetas didácticas __/__/__	Elabora todo tipo de tarjetas didácticas. Dependiendo de los intereses de tu hijo y su grado académico, pueden incluir letras del abecedario, palabras de uso frecuente, o problemas matemáticos. Puedes crearlas tú mismo con marcadores o en una computadora. Sugiérele que te ayude a cortar imágenes de revistas y péguenlas en tarjetas de 3" x 5". Luego, busca un sitio al aire libre y repasen las tarjetas juntos.
Proyecto de despensa __/__/__	Encuentra un sitio en tu casa donde puedas almacenar víveres. Puede ser un armario o un contenedor que permanezca siempre en el mismo sitio. Busca algunas latas de pintura limpias o baldes. Llénalos con todo tipo de materiales para hacer manualidades. Además de las clásicas pinturas, marcadores, papel, tijeras y pegamento, puedes incluir artículos inusuales, tales como azulejos, flores artificiales y papel de regalo. De este modo, cada vez tú y tu hijo quieran hacer una manualidad, pueden acceder a todo lo necesario en ese preciso momento.
Colecciona algún objeto __/__/__	Deja que tu hijo escoja objetos para coleccionar que sean gratuito o de bajo costo, tales como clips o botones. Si desea coleccionar algo inviable, tal como caballos, busquen imágenes en revistas o catálogos y sugiérele que los recorte y comience una colección de imágenes.
Viaje al supermercado __/__/__	En lugar de que el viaje al supermercado sea una obligación, transfórmalo en un desafío. Incluso los niños que aún no leen pueden ayudar a encontrar los artículos en los estantes. Comienza por darle a tu hijo su propia lista de compras. Revisen la lista antes de partir. Si aún no lee, puedes recortar las imágenes que aparecen en los anuncios. Muchos comercios poseen pequeños carros de compras que puedes ofrecerle para que llene el suyo propio. Cuando lleguen a un pasillo donde sepas que hay algún artículo presente en su lista, aliéntalo a buscarlo. Puede requerir tu ayuda para acceder a algún artículo que se encuentre en un estante fuera de su alcance.
Comer el abecedario __/__/__	¿No sería divertido comer el abecedario? Durante el transcurso del verano, observen cuántas frutas y verduras pueden comer de la A a la Z. Pueden elaborar un póster o un gráfico con las letras de la A a la Z. Una vez terminado, cada vez que tu hijo coma una fruta o verdura, escríbanla junto a la letra del abecedario correspondiente. También puede realizar un dibujo de lo que ha comido.

Learning Experiences *(cont.)*

¿Cuánto cuesta? __/__/__	Si salen a comer, pide ayuda a tu hijo para obtener el total de la cuenta. Anoten el costo de la comida de cada comensal. Luego, dile que lo sume y calcule cuánto se gastó en total. Puedes modificar la actividad y volverla mucho más simple, pidiéndole que sólo calcule el costo de una entrada y un trago del menú, o el costo de tres postres. Asegúrate de redondear las cifras primero.
Búsqueda del tesoro en la naturaleza __/__/__	Salgan a caminar, vayan a un parque o realicen una excursión a las montañas. Pero antes de partir, elabora una búsqueda del tesoro para tu hijo. Puede incluir todo tipo de cosas que se puedan encontrar en la naturaleza. Asegúrate que cuente con una bolsa para guardar todo lo que encuentre (y recuerda verificar con anticipación las reglas o leyes relacionadas con la sustracción de cualquier objeto). Puedes incluir cosas tales como: una hoja con bordes puntiagudos, una roca moteada, y una ramita con dos pequeñas ramificaciones. Tómense unos minutos para observar todos los elementos que ha recolectado y táchenlos de la lista.
¡Mídelo! __/__/__	Utilizar una regla, una cinta métrica o una vara de medir, constituye un modo de descubrir la altura de las cosas. Comienza por tu hijo y averigüen qué tan alto es. Ahora, busquen otros elementos para medir y comparar. Descubran cuánto mas bajo es un libro comparado con él, o cuánto más alta es la puerta. Para medir todo aquello que no pueda ser medido con una regla, toma un hilo y estíralo alrededor del objeto. Córtalo y realiza una marca en el sitio donde termina. Luego, estíralo junto a la regla o cinta de medir y descubran su longitud. Tu hijo se sorprenderá con lo diferente que pueden lucir algunos objetos que miden lo mismo, pero poseen una forma distinta.
Realiza un viaje y lleva un diario __/__/__	Si van a realizar un viaje durante el verano, pídele a tu hijo que lleve un diario. Los niños pequeños pueden recolectar postales y pegarlas en un diario en blanco. También pueden dibujar los sitios que visitaron. Si tiene acceso a una cámara de fotos, puede armar un álbum fotográfico.
Conviértete en un científico __/__/__	Sin que tu hijo lo sepa, pon una pelota dentro de una caja y colócale la tapa. Llámalo y dile que actúe como si fuese un científico. Deberá hacer preguntas y tratar de adivinar las respuestas. Si tiene dificultades para realizar las preguntas, puedes ayudarlo. Algunas pueden ser: "¿qué crees que hay en la caja?" y "¿cómo lo sabes?". Pídele que sacuda la caja y trate de adivinarlo.

Cursive Writing Chart

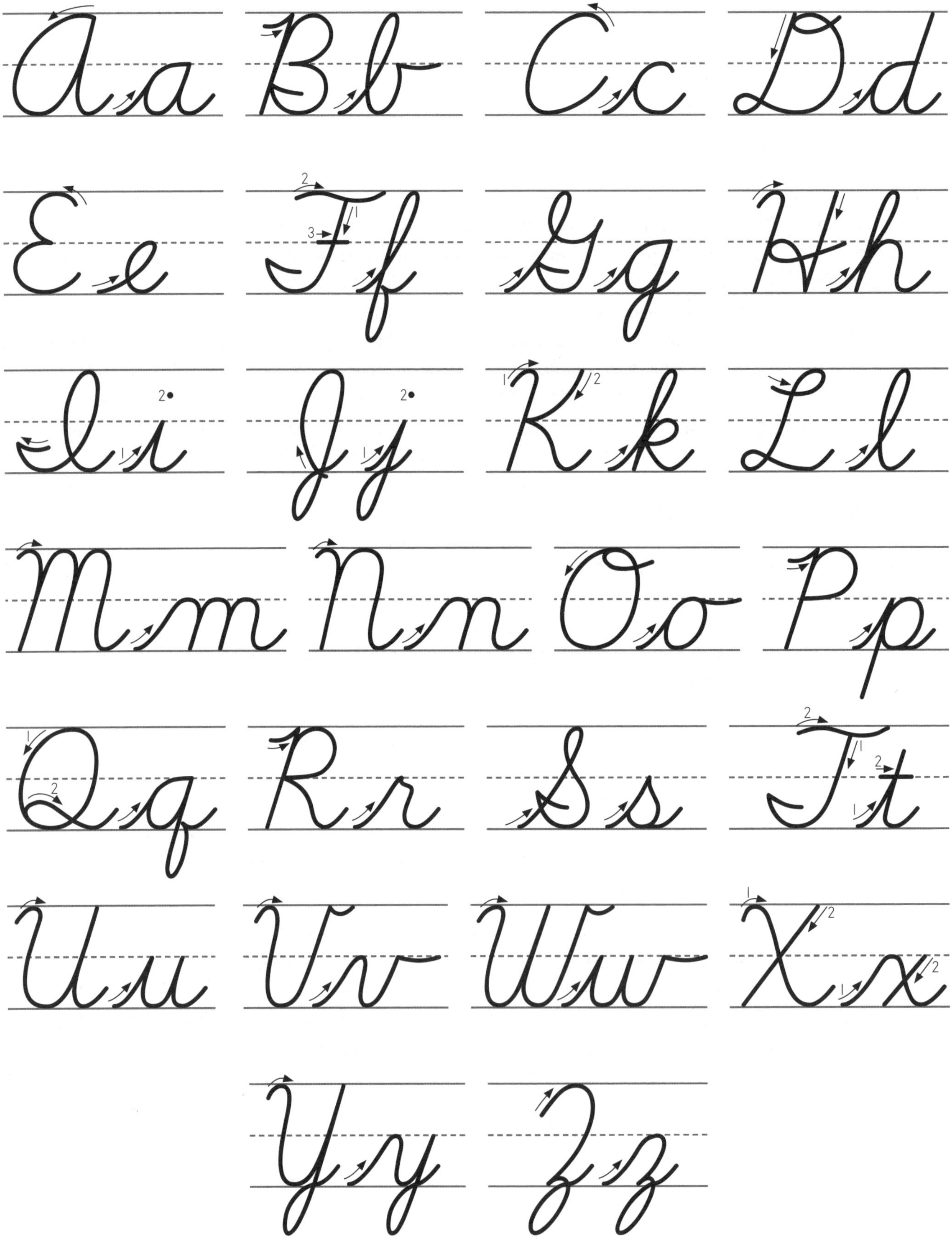

Multiplication Chart

×	0	1	2	3	4	5	6	7	8	9	10	11	12
0	0	0	0	0	0	0	0	0	0	0	0	0	0
1	0	1	2	3	4	5	6	7	8	9	10	11	12
2	0	2	4	6	8	10	12	14	16	18	20	22	24
3	0	3	6	9	12	15	18	21	24	27	30	33	36
4	0	4	8	12	16	20	24	28	32	36	40	44	48
5	0	5	10	15	20	25	30	35	40	45	50	55	60
6	0	6	12	18	24	30	36	42	48	54	60	66	72
7	0	7	14	21	28	35	42	49	56	63	70	77	84
8	0	8	16	24	32	40	48	56	64	72	80	88	96
9	0	9	18	27	36	45	54	63	72	81	90	99	108
10	0	10	20	30	40	50	60	70	80	90	100	110	120
11	0	11	22	33	44	55	66	77	88	99	110	121	132
12	0	12	24	36	48	60	72	84	96	108	120	132	144

Times Tables

1 times table

1 × 0 = 0
1 × 1 = 1
1 × 2 = 2
1 × 3 = 3
1 × 4 = 4
1 × 5 = 5
1 × 6 = 6
1 × 7 = 7
1 × 8 = 8
1 × 9 = 9
1 × 10 = 10
1 × 11 = 11
1 × 12 = 12

2 times table

2 × 0 = 0
2 × 1 = 2
2 × 2 = 4
2 × 3 = 6
2 × 4 = 8
2 × 5 = 10
2 × 6 = 12
2 × 7 = 14
2 × 8 = 16
2 × 9 = 18
2 × 10 = 20
2 × 11 = 22
2 × 12 = 24

3 times table

3 × 0 = 0
3 × 1 = 3
3 × 2 = 6
3 × 3 = 9
3 × 4 = 12
3 × 5 = 15
3 × 6 = 18
3 × 7 = 21
3 × 8 = 24
3 × 9 = 27
3 × 10 = 30
3 × 11 = 33
3 × 12 = 36

4 times table

4 × 0 = 0
4 × 1 = 4
4 × 2 = 8
4 × 3 = 12
4 × 4 = 16
4 × 5 = 20
4 × 6 = 24
4 × 7 = 28
4 × 8 = 32
4 × 9 = 36
4 × 10 = 40
4 × 11 = 44
4 × 12 = 48

5 times table

5 × 0 = 0
5 × 1 = 5
5 × 2 = 10
5 × 3 = 15
5 × 4 = 20
5 × 5 = 25
5 × 6 = 30
5 × 7 = 35
5 × 8 = 40
5 × 9 = 45
5 × 10 = 50
5 × 11 = 55
5 × 12 = 60

6 times table

6 × 0 = 0
6 × 1 = 6
6 × 2 = 12
6 × 3 = 18
6 × 4 = 24
6 × 5 = 30
6 × 6 = 36
6 × 7 = 42
6 × 8 = 48
6 × 9 = 54
6 × 10 = 60
6 × 11 = 66
6 × 12 = 72

Times Tables *(cont.)*

7 times table

7 × 0 = 0
7 × 1 = 7
7 × 2 = 14
7 × 3 = 21
7 × 4 = 28
7 × 5 = 35
7 × 6 = 42
7 × 7 = 49
7 × 8 = 56
7 × 9 = 63
7 × 10 = 70
7 × 11 = 77
7 × 12 = 84

8 times table

8 × 0 = 0
8 × 1 = 8
8 × 2 = 16
8 × 3 = 24
8 × 4 = 32
8 × 5 = 40
8 × 6 = 48
8 × 7 = 56
8 × 8 = 64
8 × 9 = 72
8 × 10 = 80
8 × 11 = 88
8 × 12 = 96

9 times table

9 × 0 = 0
9 × 1 = 9
9 × 2 = 18
9 × 3 = 27
9 × 4 = 36
9 × 5 = 45
9 × 6 = 54
9 × 7 = 63
9 × 8 = 72
9 × 9 = 81
9 × 10 = 90
9 × 11 = 99
9 × 12 = 108

10 times table

10 × 0 = 0
10 × 1 = 10
10 × 2 = 20
10 × 3 = 30
10 × 4 = 40
10 × 5 = 50
10 × 6 = 60
10 × 7 = 70
10 × 8 = 80
10 × 9 = 90
10 × 10 = 100
10 × 11 = 110
10 × 12 = 120

11 times table

11 × 0 = 0
11 × 1 = 11
11 × 2 = 22
11 × 3 = 33
11 × 4 = 44
11 × 5 = 55
11 × 6 = 66
11 × 7 = 77
11 × 8 = 88
11 × 9 = 99
11 × 10 = 110
11 × 11 = 121
11 × 12 = 132

12 times table

12 × 0 = 0
12 × 1 = 12
12 × 2 = 24
12 × 3 = 36
12 × 4 = 48
12 × 5 = 60
12 × 6 = 72
12 × 7 = 84
12 × 8 = 96
12 × 9 = 108
12 × 10 = 120
12 × 11 = 132
12 × 12 = 144

Clocks

These 12 clocks show every time to the quarter hour.

12:15

1:15

2:15

3:15

4:15

5:15

6:15

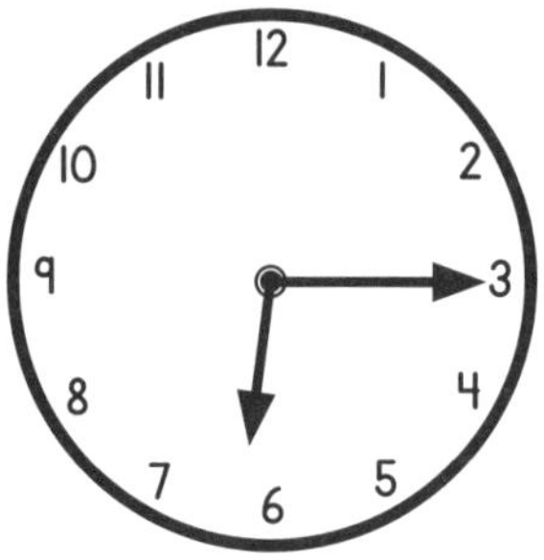

7:15

8:15

9:15

10:15

11:15

Clocks *(cont.)*

These 12 clocks show every time a quarter to the hour.

12:45

1:45

2:45

3:45

4:45

5:45

6:45

7:45

8:45

9:45

10:45

11:45

Proofreading Marks

Editor's Mark	Meaning	Example
≡	capitalize	they fished in lake tahoe.
/	make it lowercase	Five Students missed the Bus.
sp.	spelling mistake	The day was clowdy and cold.
⊙	add a period	Tomorrow is a holiday⊙
ℓ	delete (remove)	One person knew the the answer.
∧	add a word	Six ∧pups were in the litter.
∧,	add a comma	He planted peas∧, corn, and squash.
~	reverse words or letters	An otter swam in the bed kelp.
∨’	add an apostrophe	The child∨’s bike was blue.
∨“ ∨”	add quotation marks	∨“Why can't I go?∨” she cried.
#	make a space	He ate two red#apples.
‿	close the space	Her favorite game is soft ball.
¶	begin a new paragraph	to know.¶Next on the list

Answer Key

Page 12
Hidden word: GO

Page 13
3. not happy
4. don't trust
5. not like
6. don't agree
7. not believable
8. before the test
9. before school
10. don't like

Page 14
1. 778
2. 413
3. 233
4. 491
5. 506
6. 342
7. 700 + 60 + 5
8. 500 + 50 + 7
9. 100 + 80 + 6
10. 900 + 10 + 4
11. 200 + 20 + 5
12. 700 + 1
13. one hundred twenty-nine
14. three hundred sixty-five
15. seven hundred ninety
16. six hundred sixty-one

Page 15
1. I had my birthday on a Tuesday in April.
2. We will take a trip on a Monday in June.
3. The first Friday in October will be on the sixth.
4. Aunt Lisa's favorite book is Charlotte's Web.
5. My sister wanted to read a book called Press Here.
6. The funniest character in Toy Story 4 is named Forky.

Page 16
2. 254 two hundred fifty-four
3. 165 one hundred sixty-five
4. 523 five hundred twenty-three
5. 436 four hundred thirty-six
6. 312 three hundred twelve
7. 654 six hundred fifty-four
8. 125 one hundred twenty-five

Smallest number: 125
Largest number: 654

Page 17
1. Tracy packed her coat.
2. Tracy packed her socks.
3. Tracy packed her pajamas.
4. Tracy packed her journal.
5. Tracy fell asleep.

Page 18
Ones-place barrel: 1, 3, 4, 7, 8
Tens-place barrel: 10, 37, 41, 83, 99
Hundreds-place barrel: 142, 291, 296, 429, 629

Page 19
1. The cat curled up on the cushion and cried.
2. One Saturday, a silly snake slithered in the dirt.
3. Two tiny turtles walked to the city.
4. The cold wind whipped past the lake.
5. The rain poured down on the pavement.
6. The bear ate berries for breakfast.

Page 20
Total number of blocks: 36

Page 21

U	M	D	U	R	D	E	T	F	S	C	T	T
N	B	W	E	N	I	H	E	U	D	O	O	T
D	O	R	U	D	R	Z	R	F	W	O	F	U
E	U	O	E	E	I	P	W	E	T	K	M	V
R	F	K	W	C	R	C	N	D	S	E	T	Q
S	G	W	P	I	O	K	E	J	X	D	U	P
T	H	N	S	T	B	G	D	D	D	R	A	N
O	B	E	A	D	E	D	N	E	T	E	R	P
O	D	U	K	S	U	C	I	I	K	R	N	A
D	G	S	L	L	T	L	A	D	Z	S	G	V
H	C	L	A	P	P	E	D	U	R	E	A	N
E	V	U	Y	E	D	P	D	H	G	O	D	A
M	J	J	R	T	O	G	R	O	F	H	V	G
A	L	E	F	T	R	O	E	M	A	C	T	E

Answer Key *(cont.)*

Page 22

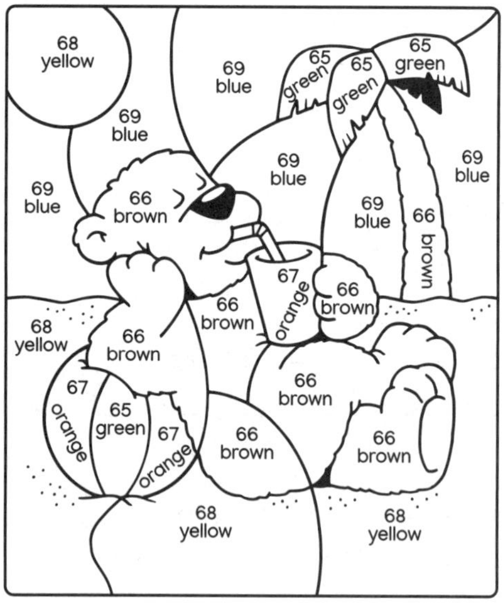

Page 23

2. "Line up at the door," said Mrs. Johnson.
3. Mom yelled, "Go, Cobras, go!"
4. Sheila wondered, "Should I wear my blue dress?"
5. My dad said, "You look nice today."
6. James asked, "May I have a glass of milk?"
7. "Please answer the phone," whispered my mother.
8. Kelly exclaimed, "Look out!"
9. "My lizard escaped," replied Henry sadly.
10. Juliette said, "I hope you can come over to play."

Page 24

1. 52
2. 70
3. 80
4. 50
5. 72
6. 35

Page 25

3. having a lot of wonder
4. having a lot of care
5. being happy
6. being soft
7. having a lot of color
8. having a lot of joy
9. being lonely
10. having a lot of harm

Page 26

2. 603
3. 613
4. 633
5. 930
6. 900

Page 27

Answers may vary.

1. nibbled
2. devoured
3. stomped
4. gasped
5. glanced
6. stared
7. paced
8. gazed
9. tiptoed
10. strolled

Page 28

One sample solution is noted below:

Row 1: **36**, **38**, 31

Row 2: **37**, 33, **35**

Row 3: **32**, **34**, 39

Page 29

1. She wore a red dress to school.
2. I can't wait for Christmas.
3. Shelly's new dog ate breakfast.
4. Daisies are pretty.
5. I wonder if I can go get pizza after the show.

Page 30

Top row: 84, 85, 83, 84

Bottom row: 83, 80, 87, 86, 81

Word: a crocodile

Page 32

1. (+)912 or (–)648
2. (+)54 or (–)24
3. (+)1,339 or (–)525
4. (+)602 or (–)508
5. (+)400 or (–)224
6. (+)120 or (–)26
7. (+)2,901 or (–)2,707
8. (+)136 or (–)38
9. (+)1,197 or (–)89

Page 33

nose, nose, roll, hang, back, hognose

Answer Key *(cont.)*

Page 34

2. (32 – 4) + (49 – 7) = 70
3. (72 – 9) + (24 – 8) = 79
4. (56 – 7) + (64 – 8) = 105
5. (36 – 6) + (35 – 7) = 58

Page 35

Answers will vary for 2–3. Possible meanings:

2. correct, right (direction)
3. remaining, left (direction)
4. put up
5. get rid of someone from work
6. put clothes in a suitcase

Page 36

1. 10
2. 1
3. 12
4. 50
5. 30
6. 31
7. 70
8. 33
9. 63
10. 11
11. 48
12. 20
13. 60
14. 21
15. 20

Page 37

1. They are sisters. They woke up in the same house and talked about "Mom."
2. They don't want to wake up Mom.
3. Answers may vary, but it is probably Mom's birthday.
4. She probably enjoys it.
5. It is probably some kind of gardening tool.

Page 38

1. 69
2. 18
3. 35
4. 19
5. 25
6. 11

Page 39

1. tripped
2. rides
3. ate
4. stood
5. scream
6. reads
7. slept
8. slipped
9. run
10. breathed

Page 40

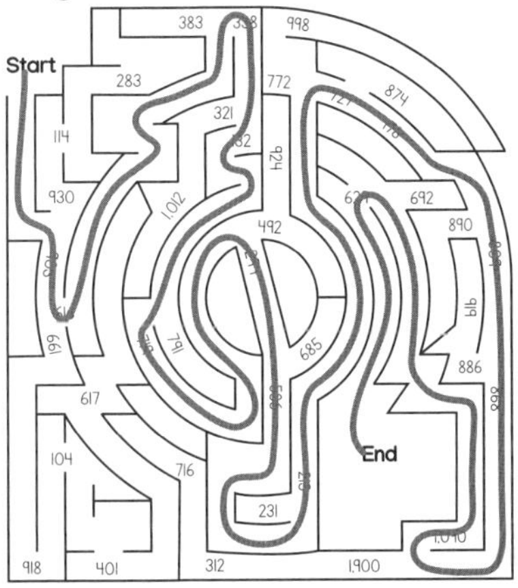

Page 41

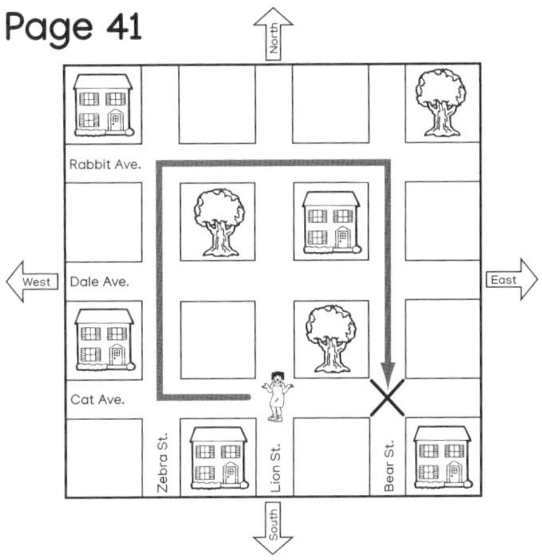

Page 42

1. 2 + 2 + 2 + 2 = 8
2. 4 × 2 = 8
3. 5 + 5 = 10
4. 2 × 5 = 10
5. 4 + 4 + 4 = 12
6. 3 × 4 = 12
7. 1 + 1 + 1 + 1 + 1 + 1 = 6
8. 6 × 1 = 6

Page 43

2. red—licorice
3. angry—man
4. interesting—story
5. long—letters

Answer Key *(cont.)*

Page 44

×	0	1	2	3	4	5	6	7	8	9	10
0	0	0	0	0	0	0	0	0	0	0	0
1	0	1	2	3	4	5	6	7	8	9	10
2	0	2	4	6	8	10	12	14	16	18	20
3	0	3	6	9	12	15	18	21	24	27	30
4	0	4	8	12	16	20	24	28	32	36	40
5	0	5	10	15	20	25	30	35	40	45	50
6	0	6	12	18	24	30	36	42	48	54	60
7	0	7	14	21	28	35	42	49	56	63	70
8	0	8	16	24	32	40	48	56	64	72	80
9	0	9	18	27	36	45	54	63	72	81	90
10	0	10	20	30	40	50	60	70	80	90	100

Page 45

2. pig–pen
3. snow–shoe
4. night–time
5. clip–board
6. shoe–lace
7. bed–time
8. play–ground
9. rain–bow
10. sun–shine

Page 46

1. 2
2. 14
3. 3
4. 1
5. 8
6. 12
7. 2
8. 2
9. 5
10. 12
11. 30
12. 16
13. 15

Page 48

1. 10
2. 5
3. 30
4. 55
5. 35
6. 50
7. 25
8. 50
9. 20
10. 45
11. 15
12. 40
13. 20
14. 55

Question: Can you multiply?

Page 50

Dots: 4
Stripes: 3
Hearts: 6
Diamonds: 5
Squares: 2

1. hearts
2. squares
3. 20

Page 51

1. Cross off 80,121; 2,157; 7,418; 102.
2. Cross off 39,643; 29,253; 144,384.
3. Cross off 879; 579.
4. Cross off 9,780.
5. Cross off 66,176.
6. 85,457

Page 52

1. 4
2. 8
3. 4
4. 6

Page 53

1. sh
2. ch
3. sh
4. sh
5. th
6. sh
7. th
8. ch
9. wh

Page 54

1. 5, 5
2. 8, 8
3. 10, 10
4. 9, 9

Page 55

2. The musician played piano, guitar, and drums.
3. I have red, blue, and green crayons.
4. I saw lions, tigers, and bears at the zoo.
5. Is this shape a triangle, square, or circle?
6. I practice on Monday, Friday, and Sunday.
7. This morning, I ate bacon, eggs, and toast.
8. I like to play soccer, golf, and tennis.

Page 56

1. 12
2. 6
3. 10

Answer Key *(cont.)*

Page 57

1. soaring
2. fluttering
3. hovering
4. swooping
5. flapping
6. gliding

Page 58

1. Each friend has 5 candies.
2. Each has 10 marbles.
3. Each friend has 3 flowers.

Page 59

1. A cat meows.
2. A duck quacks.
3. A dog woofs.
4. A sheep baas.
5. A horse neighs.
6. The wind went swoosh.
7. The thunder cracks.
8. The rain goes pitter-patter.

Page 60

2. $2 \times 1 = 2$
3. $12 \div 3 = 4$
4. $5 \times 3 = 15$ or $5 + 5 + 5 = 15$
5. $5 \times 3 = 15$ or $3 + 3 + 3 + 3 + 3 = 15$
6. $25 \div 5 = 5$
7. $12 \div 2 = 6$
8. $10 \div 5 = 2$
9. $100 \div 10 = 10$

Page 61

There are many possible answers for each.

2. flag, gate, left
3. mops, lion, spoil
4. game, come, made
5. head, fade, bean
6. thud, dust, shut
7. team, game, great
8. star, storm, story

Page 62

1. $\frac{1}{3}$
2. $\frac{4}{6}$
3. $\frac{2}{5}$
4. $\frac{3}{4}$
5. $\frac{1}{2}$
6. $\frac{1}{2}$
7. $\frac{5}{9}$
8. $\frac{1}{4}$

Page 63

1. told us to stand, read us a story
2. barked at the cat, chewed the bone
3. built a nest in the tree, is singing a song

Page 64

1. $\frac{6}{10}$
2. $\frac{2}{10}$
3. $\frac{5}{8}$
4. $\frac{7}{8}$
5. $\frac{10}{12}$
6. $\frac{10}{100}$
7. $\frac{1}{2}$
8. $\frac{20}{100}$
9. $\frac{1}{10}, \frac{1}{4}, \frac{1}{3}$
10. $\frac{3}{10}, \frac{5}{10}, \frac{8}{10}$
11. $\frac{2}{5}, \frac{2}{4}, \frac{2}{3}$
12. $\frac{1}{8}, \frac{3}{8}, \frac{7}{8}$
13. $1\frac{1}{2}, 2, 4\frac{1}{2}$
14. $\frac{1}{6}, \frac{1}{5}, \frac{1}{2}$

Page 65

1. friends
2. baby, infant
3. quietly, silently
4. shop, store
5. gift, present
6. chilly, cold

Page 66

1. $\frac{2}{4}$
2. $\frac{3}{6}$
3. $\frac{2}{3}$
4. $\frac{2}{5}$
5. $\frac{4}{6}$
6. $\frac{5}{10}$
7. $\frac{4}{10}$
8. $\frac{4}{8}$
9. $\frac{1}{3}$
10. $\frac{3}{5}$
11. $\frac{2}{5}$
12. $\frac{2}{3}$

Page 67

2. underline
3. circle
4. underline
5. circle
6. underline

Page 68

Some shapes may be divided in more than one way.

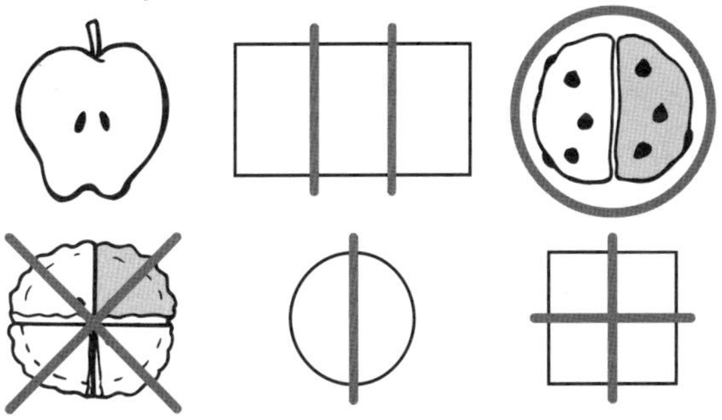

Answer Key (cont.)

Page 70

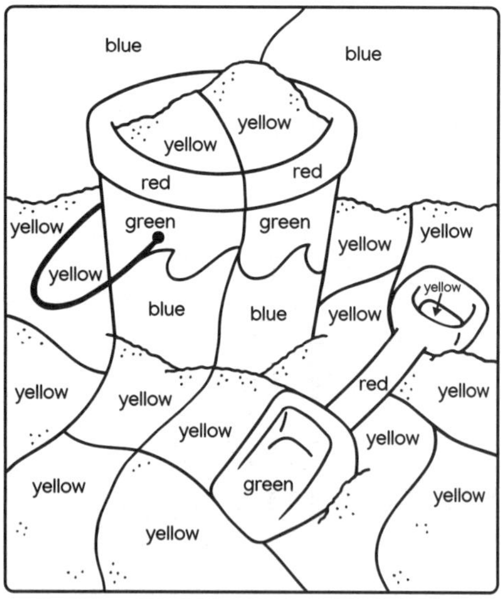

Page 71

S	W	L	E	E	W	S	T	O	R	Y
T	D	I	R	E	E	A	F	M	E	S
S	W	G	E	P	A	J	A	M	A	S
E	T	H	S	U	R	B	L	D	D	R
O	U	T	T	S	A	S	L	E	E	P
E	N	S	E	E	A	M	S	T	S	W
E	D	Y	E	T	E	D	B	A	T	H
R	E	S	O	L	C	T	E	K	A	M
S	R	E	V	O	C	S	S	E	W	E

Bonus: sweet dreams

Page 72

1. 6 marbles
2. 19 – 8 = 11 footballs
3. 9 + 7 + 5 + 3 + 7 = 31 points
4. 21 ÷ 7 = 3 tennis balls

Page 73

1. down
2. dry
3. go
4. awake
5. day
6. empty

Page 74

1. 16 + 27 = 43
2. 28 + 46 = 74
3. \$53 – \$28 = \$25
4. 83 – 65 = 18

Page 75

1. hard
2. quickly
3. intently
4. fast
5. slowly
6. loudly

Page 76

1. how much does 203 + 164 equal; 367 marbles
2. how much does 25 × 5 equal; 125 candies
3. how much does 30 ÷ 10 equal; 3 dollar bills
4. how much does \$18.89 – \$9.40 equal; \$9.49

Page 77

1. a
2. a
3. c
4. c

Page 78

2. 4 more monkeys in the tree
3. 45 cups
4. 267 books
5. 24 pencils
6. 4 flowers

Page 80

O	G	Y	R	P	B
R	P	B	G	Y	O
P	B	R	O	G	Y
G	Y	O	B	R	P
Y	O	G	P	B	R
B	R	P	Y	O	G

Page 81

Page 82

2. 150 + 130 + 210 = 490; Mariah bought about 490 party items in all.
3. 190 – 90 = 100; About 100 people said "no."
4. 210 + 320 + 60 = 590; Lucy set out about 590 jellybeans.
5. 570 – 240 = 330 – 200 = 130; The third cupcake had about 130 sprinkles.
6. 220 + 300 + 370 = 890; About 890 points were scored in all.

Page 84

Estimates will vary.

1. $1.46 + $0.60 + $0.38 + $0.52 = $2.96
2. $0.22 + $0.56 + $0.75 = $1.53
3. $1.24 + $0.43 + $0.43 + $0.52 = $2.62
4. $1.12 + $1.39 + $0.75 + $0.75 + $0.48 + $0.56 + $0.43 = $6.04

Page 85

1. *circle*: sick person, running person
2. *circle*: apple, celery

Page 86

1. 2
2. 2
3. 3
4. 4

Page 88

1. 2 pennies, 2 dimes, 1 quarter
2. 3 quarters
3. 1 penny, 1 nickel, 1 dime, 1 quarter
4. 2 half dollars
5. 2 nickels, 2 dimes, 2 quarters
6. 1 penny, 2 nickels, 4 dimes

Page 89

1. 9:00 a.m.
2. 20
3. Art
4. Mr. Castle
5. 10:45 a.m.
6. Quiet reading time

Page 90

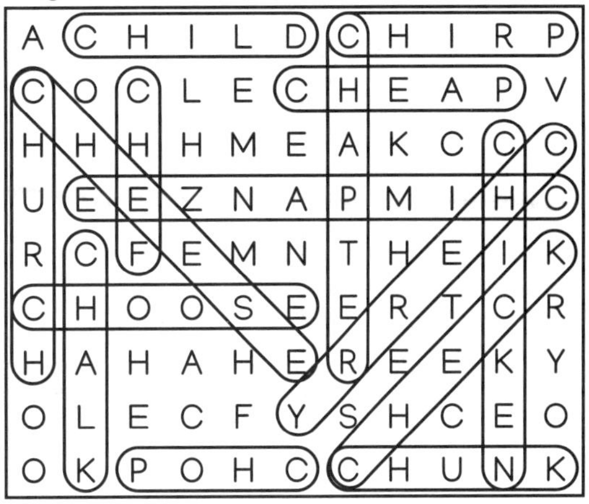

Bonus: chef

Page 91

Row 1 Across: chocolate sauce on left scoop
Row 2 Across: chocolate sprinkles
Row 3 Across: chocolate chips
Column 1 Down: drip
Column 2 Down: white spoons
Column 3 Down: black spoons

Reward Chart